CHANGES

An Oral History of
Tupac Shakur

Sheldon Pearce

SIMON & SCHUSTER

New York   London   Toronto   Sydney   New Delhi

Simon & Schuster
1230 Avenue of the Americas
New York, NY 10020

First Simon & Schuster hardcover edition June 2021

SIMON & SCHUSTER and colophon are registered trademarks of Simon & Schuster, Inc.

For information about special discounts for bulk purchases,
please contact Simon & Schuster Special Sales
at 1-866-506-1949 or business@simonandschuster.com.

The Simon & Schuster Speakers Bureau can bring authors to your live event.
For more information or to book an event, contact the Simon & Schuster Speakers Bureau
at 1-866-248-3049 or visit our website at www.simonspeakers.com.

Interior design by Ruth Lee-Mui

Manufactured in the United States of America

1   3   5   7   9   10   8   6   4   2

Library of Congress Cataloging-in-Publication Data is available.

ISBN 978-1-9821-7046-2
ISBN 978-1-9821-7048-6 (ebook)

CHORUS

(in order of appearance)

CHUCK WALKER, University of California, Davis, professor; author, *The Tupac Amaru Rebellion*

SHARONDA DAVILA-IRVING, childhood friend of Tupac and Black Panther Party daughter

JANE RHODES, University of Illinois at Chicago professor; author, *Framing the Black Panthers*

LEVY LEE SIMON, actor, 127th Street Repertory Ensemble

RICHARD PILCHER, retired principal acting teacher at Baltimore School for the Arts

BECKY MOSSING, Baltimore School for the Arts class of 1988

STELLA NAIR, University of California, Los Angeles professor

KENDRICK WELLS, friend and personal assistant

RYAN D ROLLINS, Marin City rapper, member of One Nation MCs

BARBARA OWENS, former English teacher at Tamalpais High School

PUDGEE THA PHAT BASTARD, New York City rapper

D-SHOT, Vallejo rapper, member of the Click

ROB MARRIOTT, former *Source* editor and *Vibe* writer

JUSTIN TINSLEY, *The Undefeated* staff writer

KHALIL KAIN, actor, "Raheem" in *Juice*

GOBI RAHIMI, videographer, Look Hear Creations cofounder

JAKI BROWN, casting director for *Juice*

MARK ANTHONY NEAL, African and African American studies department chair at Duke University

LESLIE GERARD, former assistant and A & R at Interscope Records

MOE Z MD, Los Angeles producer

KEVIN HOSMANN, art director and designer for *2Pacalypse Now*

KARL KANI, fashion designer

ALEX ROBERTS, former head of business affairs at Death Row Records

TIM NITZ, engineer

COLIN WOLFE, Los Angeles producer

ERIC ALTENBURGER, art director and designer for *Strictly for My N.I.G.G.A.Z...* and *Me Against the World*

BLU, Los Angeles rapper

WENDY DAY, Rap Coalition founder

ETHAN BROWN, author, *Queens Reigns Supreme*

TERRENCE "KLEPT" HARDING, Brooklyn rapper, Junior M.A.F.I.A. member

EZI CUT, Danish DJ and producer

CHARISSE JONES, former *New York Times* staff writer; *USA Today* correspondent; coauthor of *Shifting: The Double Lives of Black Women in America*

RICHARD DEVITT, juror in Tupac's sexual abuse case

CATHY SCOTT, former *Las Vegas Sun* crime reporter; author, *The Killing of Tupac Shakur*

DR. LEON PACHTER, former trauma department chief at Bellevue Hospital

GREG KADING, former LAPD detective

ANGELA ARDIS, Tupac pen pal; author, *Inside a Thug's Heart*

VIRGIL ROBERTS, former president of SOLAR Records

TOMMY "D" DAUGHERTY, former Death Row Records engineer

CORMEGA, New York City rapper

NAHSHON ANDERSON, former Look Hear Creations intern

ERIC FARBER, former attorney for the Tupac estate

DR. JOHN FILDES, former trauma department chief at Las Vegas's University Medical Center

CHUCK WALKER *Initially, he wasn't that big a hero in colonial Peru. The Spanish were so petrified they really tamped down on, like, publicity. It's really the twentieth century, and particularly with this really peculiar 1968 military government that is leftist.*

This is a moment when US-supported right-wing military regimes are dominating. Peru has a left-wing regime. And they're looking for a hero. He becomes the national symbol. He's indigenous but mestizo—so in other words, he's got European blood. He's cool looking. He's got a ponytail. He looks good on a horse. The other national heroes had all been white dudes from the coast.

So in the sixties, people wrote more about him. What I understood is the Black Panthers chapter that Afeni was involved with in New York City had a reading group, and they were understandably looking for revolutionaries of color. They read about Túpac Amaru II and thought it was cool. Afeni said later that she named her son that because she wanted him to be worldly.

I

SHARONDA DAVILA-IRVING In our community, we would be considered extended family. Our mothers were pregnant together.* We were born together. Our mothers were both in the Black Panther Party. When we were small, my family moved to Jersey City. So when we saw each other, we were going there or coming here. We were taught to be leaders from the beginning. When you don't really know boundaries, in a positive sense, being amongst the people is important to your existence. If your parents are immersed in working for the people, then that means as a kid, you're right there with whoever they are going to visit or whoever they are going to support. You play with all the kids that are there.

JANE RHODES The founding of the Panthers is very much rooted to the dual sort of transitions of both civil rights and Black Power activism during that period. They're very much indebted to and engaged with the sort of rising Black nationalist thinking and affinity that's coming out of SNCC† in particular, but also Malcolm X in the Nation of Islam. Robert Williams.‡ There's a whole constellation of people who they sort of saw and heard and read.

Both Huey Newton and Bobby Seale, who are

*In 1970, Afeni Shakur was tried as a member of the Panther 21 for 186 counts of attempted murder, attempted arson, and conspiracy to blow up schools, police precincts, department stores, and the New York Botanical Garden. Tupac was conceived while she was out on bail. While pregnant, she defended herself and others at trial, and a month after her acquittal, on June 16, 1971, Tupac was born.

†The Student Nonviolent Coordinating Committee, a student action committee that challenged segregation in the 1960s.

‡Civil rights leader and president of the Monroe, North Carolina, chapter of the NAACP who obtained a charter from the NRA to establish a Black rifle club and fight off the KKK.

ostensibly the founders of the Black Panthers, sort of came up in the kind of civil rights, Black community activism of the period. They worked for antipoverty agencies. Bobby Seale was a Vietnam War vet. And so he was very much situated within that kind of antiwar veterans movement. They both are going to Merritt College, which is a junior college, and they get caught up in all of the stuff that's going on. All of this is going on simultaneously. It's just this maelstrom of activism. It's not surprising that this would happen in Oakland and San Francisco, in particular. Those cities kind of epitomize the crisis and the grievances of young Black people. The urban renewal and the rising inequality and the destruction of the postwar promise had struck a chord.

At Merritt College, they are part of a Black student group called the Student Advisory Committee. They meet each other, and they're both sort of underwhelmed by the sort of activist potential of their colleagues at the college. They felt like it's not radical enough, it's not militant enough. They wanted to really push for a much more sort of strident and militant kind of activism. One of the things that they did was they took it outside, away from the academy. They're sort of straddling class. They have the benefit of being well read and much more educated than a lot of the people around them. But they still are deeply identified with the brothers on the street. That very much shapes, I think, the underlying ideology of the party. Basically, they organize by pulling together some friends, a small group; there are just eight or nine folks that are sitting around debating, coming up with kind of grandiose ideas, but not really doing much.

Then the prototypical story: a young Black man is

killed by the police in nearby Richmond,* and the parents of the young man sort of appealed to this group of activists and said, "Hey, would you help us?" And so this is the founding story, if you will, because they get mobilized and actually have a purpose and start organizing. They organize demonstrations at the sheriff's office; that's when they started the Black Panther newspaper. They begin to sort of articulate all of the things that are resonating in this current moment: a critique of the police and police treatment of Black people and police brutality in Black and poor communities; a critique of structural inequality. They're not that generative. They're borrowing from a lot of places. But they forge an entity, and a lot of it is about making demands and articulating those demands.

*On April 1, 1967, twenty-two-year-old Denzil Dowell of North Richmond, California, was shot and killed by police responding to a burglary report. A jury ruled it a "justifiable homicide."

The initial work was really this idea of surveillance to the police, which I think is a really interesting and a kind of genius project. They're going to reverse the gaze. It's really a way of disrupting state power. It came back to bite them in the ass, but that was sort of a key action. It appealed to the younger acolytes to join up because there's all of this anger and fury in the community about the police. Over time, they begin to see themselves as doing more, being servants of the people.

That very much comes out of reading Marxist theory, reading Milton, looking at sort of postcolonial struggles, and recognizing that part of what you have to do is win the hearts and minds of the community and try to respond to the various issues that are sort of hurting the community. The service initiatives really sort of emerge gradually, and really take off, quite frankly, after the party begins to sort of step away from or abandon the police-confrontation tactic.

SHARONDA DAVILA-IRVING Because of the targeting of the Panthers, many people's parents took different pathways out of what was imminent danger for them. Some people just walked away from it. Some people went to jail. Some people just stopped and went mainstream, because it just was too hard to keep going. Some people got hooked on drugs, because of the level of stress and anxiety. But their kids came out differently with gifts that their parents instilled in them. He was able to really be prepared to shine so that when he got that opportunity, all of that grooming was paid back when it needed to be.

JANE RHODES If you look at the people that really found the Panthers compelling, it's urban youth, primarily Black youth, but they had a lot of other people of color and white allies who were also drawn to them. It's about the deep inequalities and crisis of the city in this historical moment. The Vietnam War has a powerful role here because you have a whole generation that is completely sort of disillusioned by the state. This generation increasingly sees themselves in solidarity with sort of global movements. It's not surprising that an organization comes along that takes a very different approach from the civil rights movement, that says, "We're not asking for our rights, we're going to demand them," that's uncompromising, that lays out not only a social justice agenda but also an agenda that really critiques the entire structure of capitalism, and the ways in which capitalism and racism operate in tandem. I think all of that spoke to not only Black folks but a lot of young people. It was more than just marching and protesting. You could feed people, you could educate people, you could help families with incarcerated family members, you could provide health care. And I think that's a powerful thing, particularly for young people who feel like they don't have a way to actually sort of serve their community or address the pain that they see.

The Panthers were extraordinarily skilled at creating an image and a persona. They were attractive. People wanted to be them. I was in junior high school when the Panthers were founded, and my brother was in the Panthers, so I've lived through that moment. And, you know, the Panthers were hot shit. They had sex appeal, they were rhetorically incredibly skilled. Eldridge Cleaver or Bobby Seale or Huey Newton or Kathleen Cleaver could stand in front of a microphone and just lay it out in extraordinary and exquisitely articulate detail. I think they were a profound contrast to the heroes of the civil rights movement.

SHARONDA DAVILA-IRVING If you talk to children of Panthers, you will probably hear some similar things around developing the mind and developing the ability to go into a room and speak to anybody. Across communities, we've got certain principles that are shared within the party, and it makes us, I think, a unique group of people. The world got an opportunity to see an example of what our parents were trying to create for their kids and for all Black kids with Tupac.

JANE RHODES I think they understood that the news media in particular was oriented toward sensationalism. And they knew that they would get attention for being sensational. And so they sort of delivered that. And what that did over time was to create a cult of personality, really, for the entire organization. So at the same time that the state is demonizing them, and trying to undermine them, and going after them guns blazing, the popular media—you know, quite frankly, the Panthers sold. Before I was an academic, I was a journalist, and if it bleeds, it leads. That's the premise. So they were a commodity, a saleable commodity, and the Panthers knew that. They were like, *Okay, I'll give you something*, and then they would deliver the goods.

The sort of younger members of the press and other media organizations . . . some of them were part of that world that was enamored of the Panthers. Tom Wolfe's classic send-up of the Panthers* was very much about that: young, white, upper-middle-class liberals wanted to get in with the Panthers. It was a way for them to define and deploy their political leanings—to get street cred, essentially. And so that certainly played into the media fascination.

*Wolfe's June 1970 article "Radical Chic: That Party at Lenny's" for *New York* magazine explored the co-opting of radical causes by white socialites.

The Panthers were very strategic. Kathleen Cleaver told me, "We stayed in the face of the media because that was one strategy for not getting killed." They courted that media attention, and they knew that it would be far more difficult for them to be incarcerated or killed by the state if they had that kind of following.

The parallels are kind of unmistakable. It doesn't necessarily mean that the rhetoric and the tactics are the same. But the conditions are very similar. And I think that the same thing that helped mobilize young people into the streets and into protest movements in the sixties and early seventies is very much in action today.

SHARONDA DAVILA-IRVING Growing up around the Black Panther Party created a sense that anything was possible for me. You're with people who are doing all kinds of things—the poets, the musicians. And Pac was a creative person.

LEVY LEE SIMON The history of the African American studio 127th Street Repertory Ensemble, founded by the great Ernie McClintock, started I think in the 1960s with Lou Gossett. Lou Gossett went on to pursue his career in Hollywood, and Ernie was the one that was left to develop the company. He felt like there were particular needs that the African American theater artists had that were not being addressed in a white theater. So he wanted to accentuate that in teaching acting from that point of view.

I graduated from Cheyney State College in Pennsylvania in the early eighties, and at twenty-two, I decided I wanted to pursue a career in acting. I'm from Harlem. When I came back home, back then the face of Black theater was the Negro Ensemble Company with Douglas Turner Ward, and all of those great actors that came out of there.* But there was this buzz around town about Ernie. I met a couple of people that sang his praises and told me that their work was more cutting edge and provocative, and I was all about that. Intuitively, I just felt like, *You know what, I'm gonna check these people out.*

*Alumni include Angela Bassett, Laurence Fishburne, Samuel L. Jackson, Phylicia Rashad, Denzel Washington, and Billy Dee Williams.

I auditioned and got in, and the great thing about Ernie's company was that it was like a training ground. Once you're in a company, then you did vocal training, you did speech and diction, you did movement. We did all kinds of different scene-study exercises and acting exercises. He had this concept: that his ensemble should be trained together, so that when they stepped on the stage, they would be a unified force.

We did a play called *Hand Is on the Gate*, which was an ensemble piece that was a collection of poems by Langston Hughes that we dramatized. We did a play where we told the story of Malcolm X through his speeches. Then, in 1984, Ernie came in and told us that we were going to do *A Raisin in the Sun* at the Apollo Theater as part of [a fundraiser] for Jesse Jackson, who was running for president back then.

Jesse was going to speak at intermission, and we were going to be the entertainment for the night. Minnie Gentry, who had played Mama on Broadway with Sidney Poitier, was gonna play Mama in the show. And then there was a young Tupac Shakur.

He was twelve years old, and no one knew what was in his future, but he played my son, Travis. His mother had been bringing him around the company. There were a number of kids around during that time. Terrence Howard, Minnie Gentry's [great-]grandson, would come hang out and watch, and Bokeem Woodbine, son of Mamie Anderson, who was in a company, would come through and watch and study. But Tupac—whatever that "it factor" is that people talk about, the indescribable thing that certain performers or artists have, he had it. He already had it back then.

SHARONDA DAVILA-IRVING When you're a teenager and your personality starts to become a little bit more distinct— He was a sensitive guy, which allowed for us to be able to really kind of share experiences with one another in a way that you don't always necessarily talk to everybody about. What people see as celebrity, I just see as family. You could be creative and dynamic and outgoing, but you also were a part of the family, so go sit your ass down.

We spent a lot of our time talking. We went to the movies and to the beach and got on the train and went places. My aunt would take us places; she was the one with the car. It was a fancy sports car. So we would be excited to go places with her in her car. When you talk to people who were a part of his life from earlier on, I feel like the political landscape of the time is inextricable from what we were doing and saying. It is hard to understand that it really was a way of life. If we were doing something, we didn't know if we were there because they were trying to organize a rent strike or something. It wasn't like, "Oh, let's hook up and go to Great Adventure."

LEVY LEE SIMON After we did the performance at the Apollo, later that summer, we did an entire summer at the Walden School.* They had a great theater off of Central Park West. We did an ensemble of plays where every time he would step on the stage there would be an audible reaction from the audience, just for him stepping on the stage. I mean, he just had this thing. He was twelve then.

Pac was a knucklehead. He was laughing all the time, cracking jokes, playing pranks on people. He would terrorize the women just doing practical jokes. One day, he got into the women's dressing room and he stole somebody's big panties, they were like big bloomers, and he put them on his head and he was running around the theater.

But then, on a more serious note, he later had a birthday and we collected money for his birthday, so he could get a birthday gift. Everybody in the company chipped in. Afeni was going through her problems with substances at

*A progressive Manhattan private school in operation from 1914 until 1988 whose students included Mike Nichols, Matthew Broderick, and Michael Diamond of the Beastie Boys.

that time, and so he took that money and he went grocery shopping for his family. He was selfless like that. He wasn't thinking about himself, he was thinking about his family, his sister, his mama.

SHARONDA DAVILA-IRVING We hung out and we had fun, but because we didn't get to see each other every day, when we did, it would be a whole occasion for me and him. My aunt would either get me or get him and bring them over or whatever. But it would be like a whole day or a whole weekend of stuff; it would be like an adventure. We would always make time to catch up around what was going on in our little preteen lives. For us, it was deep because we were immersed in a community with family members who were doing a lot of social stuff. And also, as we got older, times were changing. And as times changed, the movement changed, and as the movement changed, our experiences as young people changed. We did a lot of talking around how shit was different.

He was protective of the people that he loved. I think that he understood that the journey that he was on was going to be something that would be big enough to really create a community or continue a community.

LEVY LEE SIMON I think that being a part of the ensemble helped shape him. But I also think it had to do with growing up in New York City and having to be the man of the house at the time. Taking responsibility. He took responsibility for his family. So there was that side of him, underneath all of everything, that was very, very serious. Plus, having a mother like Afeni. It wasn't just about her issues with substances. She also, don't forget, was one of the Panther 21. He was raised with that. Afeni was a powerful, powerful presence.

SHARONDA DAVILA-IRVING At that time, that's like the early, early stages of hip-hop. Regionalism plays a part in it, too, because if you were in New York, at that time, you were rewinding songs, practicing, and learning the lyrics. I had an older brother and we wanted to be just like him. We were probably trying to figure out what was cool based on what my brother was doing, which meant getting into rap.

As I'm thinking about it, I don't know if, as we were rapping and singing the stuff that was on the radio, was he in the back of his mind like, *Oh, yeah, I can do this.* But it's hard to think of any crystallizing hip-hop moment because it's all baked into the time. I started to see a distinct creative side to him once he went to art school in Baltimore.

LEVY LEE SIMON He hung out with us until maybe fifteen or sixteen, somewhere near when he left to go to Baltimore.

SHARONDA DAVILA-IRVING It was a surprise to me when they moved to Baltimore. We rode with them down there. Afeni probably told them they were moving, but I didn't know until they came with the car. It was exciting. He was excited. But also, it was like, *What is life gonna be like outside of New York?* He's still a young kid, basically, having his whole life uprooted to an entirely different place. So there's this sense of having no clue what comes next. We thought Baltimore was the country. "You 'bout to move all the way to *Baltimore*?" The idea of somebody moving—you kind of know: *I don't know when I might see you again*, especially when you're a kid. Baltimore was definitely not the landing place. But all of that rap stuff really happened once he got there. Us growing up, that wasn't how I viewed him or how I looked at him, or even how his swag was. The rap thing came about after.

CHUCK WALKER *The Bourbon Reforms were a series of measures of increased taxes. Basically, the Spanish were losing hegemony to France and England, and they were cranking up the tax machine for the Americas. And so it hit everyone really hard. Indigenous people had to work in the mines. They had to pay a head tax. And those were sort of bad years, those years. There were some climate problems. So it got harder and harder to pay off the taxes. But it wasn't just fiscal. They wanted to get rid of the office called the cacique, which was this ethnic authority. They wanted neutral people for the role, not traditional people. They wanted to name their own people, and Túpac Amaru II and others rose up in response. It was a growing crescendo of exploitation and frustration.*

II

RICHARD PILCHER I came in the first year that BSA* was full-time. The previous year, in 1980, they had an after-school program, and there were a few teachers, but it opened to students full-time in 1981. I was there then as a principal acting teacher, and I remained that until I retired fully a couple years ago. The idea when the school was set up was that working professionals would teach the students. This was unique and still remains unique, frankly, across the country—that the majority of the teachers were adjunct faculty. I was adjunct for about the first nineteen years and then I went full-time. So everybody who was teaching was also working in their profession at the same time.

I think this gave and continues to give the school a really unique flavor. It really did not have some of the hierarchies and groups that ordinary high schools have. For instance, there's no jock culture there. There are no teams. Your status in the school is pretty much based on how good you are at your art form. And so students who were good dancers or good artists or musicians or actors or whatever, they tended to be in the sort of in-crowd.

There was quite a fair amount of tolerance in the school, I think. Certainly it was racially inclusive. At least

*In 1979, the Baltimore School for the Arts was created by a school board resolution as part of the Baltimore City school system with the purpose of preparing art students for professional careers.

50 percent of the school at any given time is African American and other people of color. That lent kind of a unique quality to the school. I mean, there were students there who would never have met each other if they'd gone to their neighborhood schools. There were friendships that grew up—between straight and gay, Black and white—that just never would have happened. In fact, while he was at BSA, Tupac's closest friend was a white male.

In many ways, it was a kind of a home for outsiders—for students that, because of their creativity and sensitivity and artistic talents, were often not fully accepted in their regular high schools. No place is perfect. Certainly I'm sure that there were conflicts and cliques. That's sort of inevitable. But in the main, there was a tremendous amount of acceptance of differences.

BECKY MOSSING BSA was this unbelievable new place, and we were very, very open with one another. It was a utopia, and every possible day, we looked at each other as artists, we were treated like artists. I think that people at BSA really felt like things were moving forward in terms of equality—that things were improving. What we have talked about since, especially in today's world, is what happened when we all left: culture shock. Every single one of us felt it when we left.

I have a really close friend who was in the same class as me, so we were both a year ahead of Tupac, and he actually wound up going to jail for armed robbery, along with another classmate of Tupac—they were in the same ensemble. They just got out this spring, serving twenty-six years of a fifty-four-year sentence. My friend came from an area in Baltimore that was incredibly impoverished, incredibly crime-ridden, and very, very difficult. He never met a white person until he came to BSA. And one of the things that he says is he wished that BSA could have been a boarding school, and I think this is true of Tupac, too, because coming into the building and then leaving and having to make a switch and going back into your neighborhood was a challenge.

RICHARD PILCHER I have a memory of either Tupac telling me, or someone who knew Tupac telling me, he had been raised to believe that white people were devils. That they were essentially evil. You know about his background and his mother. Then he came to BSA, and he found that that wasn't the case. There were people there who believed in him—the teachers and other students—and valued him for who he was. They weren't looking down on him at every moment of the day as an inferior second-class citizen. It was revelatory for him.

BSA is a place where a student would stand up and receive the undivided attention of a teacher for fifteen or twenty minutes or half an hour or whatever it was. That just doesn't happen in most high schools. So there was a sense that who they were was being validated—what they were doing and what they were thinking and how they were feeling. And of course, in theater, in particular, a lot of what we do has to do with exploring your feelings, your inner landscape, bringing that out and making it public.

It's a very tricky thing to do in high school. High school is a time when kids basically want to hide and then come out when they're eighteen. They're sort of trying to build a persona that's keeping them safe. And then you come into a theater class and we say, "We don't get to be safe. I'm sorry, you have to show who you are, through your characters, and explore your feelings in front of us." And that's very scary.

I think what we tried and tried and tried to create was a kind of a safe space where students could be themselves. And I think more often than not, we succeeded, at least to some degree, and I think that Tupac was able to stand up in front of us and his peers in a way that he just wouldn't have been able to do anyplace else.

BECKY MOSSING I remember being in homeroom, which was in the ballroom of the school, and seeing this kid with his pick in his hair and his wifebeater and jeans and this huge smile, these sparkling teeth. It's so cliché to say, but he had this light around him. He had this magnetism. I remember sitting back and thinking, *Who is that kid? He's new and people are already drawn to him like he's been here for years.*

We had homeroom together. We had lunch together. School was really small. The theater department was really small. And so we were often together. We had movement classes that were, like, some dance, but more like exploratory movement and how that connected to acting. There were voice classes and musical theater, but the musical theater classes came in your junior year, so he had those during his last year at BSA.

And then we had pretty intense acting classes with two very specific teachers: Richard Pilcher, who did a lot of Shakespeare, and Donald Hicken, who is the head of the program. Tupac would have worked with Richard quite intensely during his first and second years doing scene work, monologue work, theater games.

RICHARD PILCHER He was a really nice kid. People say, "Wait a minute, you mean this guy with a thug tattoo and a pissed-off persona?" I really liked him. He was funny. He was essentially very sweet, very sensitive. I think certainly there was some anger there, although I never really saw it come out. I mean, it was a sense of injustice that he was keenly aware of—how his family, how his people, if you will, have been treated. Highly justifiable. But that wasn't the primary thing I saw.

We really connected I think mostly in Shakespeare. He, not surprisingly, because of his gift for language, fell in love with Shakespeare. He wasn't really familiar with it before that, but he had a real talent for it; he had a great sense for the rhythm and music of the verse. He obviously took that love for words and language in a different direction, but he was very charismatic. He had those eyes that just conveyed a whole lot.

And he had a very good, muscular physique. The dance department sort of glommed onto him and used him whenever they could. There's not really any official crossover between theater and dance now, but in the early days we had more classes that could be perhaps combined; it was a smaller school. I co-taught a class with a dance teacher for dancers and actors that unfortunately didn't happen anymore after a certain point because the departments just became too demanding. But Tupac went to the dance department and he danced in several productions, rehearsing after school primarily. And he was extremely popular there, particularly among the girls, as you can imagine.

BECKY MOSSING He was always flirting. But then when he had a girlfriend, he was always super honorable. And he was always, always respectful.

SHARONDA DAVILA-IRVING I remember he came up after they moved. We were sitting in my kitchen, and he was telling me about art school. He was really, really excited. And I remember being like, "Yo, this is so dope." One of the things that made him a good entertainer is that he's a good storyteller. He's a Gemini, and growing up reading and being a leader and speaking in front of people, you know how to tell a story. You know how to give the details that matter and draw the audience. He was telling me about his classes. He did the little acting exercise that he was learning. It was, like, super exciting, because you could see that, like—something good is happening out of this.

RICHARD PILCHER Sometimes you'll run into ego in kids—and adults, too, obviously—where they're not receptive to coaching. They're not receptive to being told, "No, this isn't working. You need to do this another way." And we've had some leave over the years because they just couldn't take it, couldn't stand being criticized. The teachers tend to be pretty gentle, but we're also direct, and there's a certain professional standard. Well, he was very open to coaching. He was a very eager learner. And he was pretty open about what he didn't know. He had a kind of vulnerability that, with a little encouragement, he would drop some of that armor. I said to the kids for years: "I don't know where you're coming from in terms of neighborhood, family life. I know that you may have to leave here and put up your armor to protect yourself. But here in this class, we need to be able to drop that armor and open up," and he was able to do that.

BECKY MOSSING During his junior year, his mother was stuck in jail, and he was living in an apartment with a college-age roommate. I never met the roommate. I think he was at the Maryland Institute College of Art because they lived right off North Avenue. He was working so he could pay his rent. He was basically paying his own rent so that he could stay in Baltimore and go to school. He worked *a lot*; most weekends, a few evenings busing tables.

SHARONDA DAVILA-IRVING That was a difficult time because his mother was really struggling. That's no secret. It's difficult to talk about. Black people, we don't put all our business out there.

I remember him just kind of explaining to me what was going on. We talked a lot about personal things, what was going on as a result of his mother. It was one of those things where you are raised in an environment where you are surrounded by people who love and nurture you and nurture all of the creative aspects of who you are, and you're in a certain type of environment, and then when you start to struggle and you are no longer in that bubble, you have to develop the other survival skills that you need, but the desire to still be creative and doing the thing that you now realize you really love, you have to figure that out, too.

BECKY MOSSING I remember him sitting on my parents' deck just quietly staring out at the woods behind our house. I don't even remember why he was out there, but he was out there by himself. It must've been the morning after a party or something, because I remember walking out to see him and seeing him sigh and looking back at me with these long-ass curly eyelashes and just sort of shaking his head and going, "Nature." And I was like, "Yeah?" And he just shrugged at me and looked back out at the woods.

RICHARD PILCHER I'm not a huge rap expert or even fan, god knows, but I have a book of his raps as poetry, and you can see that pain that he was often dealing with and how he was trying to come to terms with that. A very, very sensitive young man.

BECKY MOSSING In childhood and in middle school, no one I knew used the N-word. It was a bad, bad word. And then, all of a sudden, here's my friend Tupac using this word. What the hell? Why are you using this word? It's a horrible, derogatory term.

I remember, very, very clearly, like, saying, "Don't use that word around me."

He said, "I am taking that word back. I'm using that word to empower me and to empower my people."

My little, like, sixteen-, seventeen-year-old self, in my ignorance at the time, I couldn't even hear that. "Don't say it to me."

He said, "Okay. I won't use it around you." He did it out of respect for what I felt, that sort of visceral response that I had for that word, and still have.

I was probably wrong at that moment to say that,

but he didn't call me on that. He still had that respect for a friend's feelings.

SHARONDA DAVILA-IRVING I remember him telling me about the new friends that he was meeting out there [at BSA] and the balance of trying to maintain for the house and still trying to be creative. The dichotomy that that presents for your thinking and your being. We can talk about the art shit, the community organizations that I'm connecting with and all that, and what I'm feeling about what's going on in my house. But I gotta be over here, really making sure that everybody is okay.

BECKY MOSSING Often, as an acting teacher, I talk about innate giftedness. I talk about innate presence. Those are not things that you can teach. You can teach process, you can teach craft. You cannot teach that kind of magnetism. Tupac understood how to harness energy and bring people along for the ride. It was something that he just had; he was born with it. But he also was so incredibly smart and so incredibly malleable. So, when he was in a class and he was working with a teacher, and the teacher gave him tools, he could then utilize all those innate gifts that he had and he was just unstoppable.

RICHARD PILCHER He loved the school. When Afeni told him they were leaving, he wept. He did not want to go. This was a kind of home for him that, I think in some ways, he never had—a place where he was really accepted.

SHARONDA DAVILA-IRVING I could tell that he was excited about California. There's like a whole different kind of vibe and an opportunity to expand his creativity in a new pocket. It was like one of those things where you are on the cusp of something really big.

BECKY MOSSING He always had a notepad with him. He would always be writing, jotting stuff down. And he was so quick-witted. I remember I would say, "Okay, here's a topic. Rap." He'd be like, "All right," and just rhyme. The words that would come out of his mouth, and the way that they would have meaning. I remember thinking, *How is it possible that anyone can have a brain that can do that?*

STELLA NAIR *It was actually very much a multiethnic group that followed him, at the same time when there's clear rhetoric about ethnicity and nationhood. For Túpac Amaru II, anybody could follow him with the understanding that they're going to kick out the Spanish and the Incas are going to take back over.*

CHUCK WALKER *His name means that he had ties to the Incas— that is, the leaders of the Incas—who were the very developed civilization that were there when the Spanish came and conquered in the sixteenth century. He had Inca bloodlines, which are really important because it gave him a lot of prestige. The people in Peru, then and even today, still venerate the Incas.*

He was a very well-educated guy, bilingual in Spanish and Quechua, the indigenous Inca language, which is the most spoken indigenous language today in the Americas. He was a really interesting guy because he could fit anywhere in society. He went out in the countryside chewing coca leaves, speaking Quechua with the indigenous people, but he was invited into the houses of the elite in Cusco. They would have talked to him about the news. He apparently knew Latin pretty well. So the context was growing taxes, growing tensions, exploitation, but then also his own ability to sort of put together a project, saying, We're going to bring back the Incas, but we're also going to keep the Catholic Church. Crazy stuff that who knows how it would have worked out in the end.

III

KENDRICK WELLS Back in the late eighties, early nineties, there were basically two or three pockets of Black
communities in Marin County. The biggest pocket was
Marin City, which was predominantly Black, and they had,
like, these tall buildings, which were housing projects, and
then they had these lower-level buildings with more typical
projects. These were all built for the shipyard workers of
the sixties. Marin City was basically the stronghold. Then
you also had the San Rafael area, which was about four
miles north, where they had more housing for the influx
of Asian and Mexican immigrants that came in during that
whole late-eighties era. Then there were parts of Novato,
the outskirts of the richer areas. Those were your Black
communities. When people saw you in any of the outskirts
areas—like Sausalito or Mill Valley or San Rafael or Corte
Madera—they would assume you were from Marin City.

I was from Sausalito, but all my friends were in Marin
City. My father was rich, and because of me being in Sausalito, I was always picked on by the cops. I was pretty
popular for going against the grain; they said I couldn't go
to San Rafael or Mill Valley, but that's where I was because
that's where the cute girls were that liked guys like me.
And I had a car, and I was doing it. I was used to being

harassed by the police, who were trying to keep me out, but they couldn't because I was learning things to say; they were actually teaching me how to deal with them.

Tupac and his mom arrived in Marin City. Tupac was this guy who only wanted to do music. So he would get out because he and his crew would go do shows in the suburbs. They would go to house parties, block parties, wherever, and they would get out of Marin City. Not that we were trying to escape Marin City, but there was more to see. Our names kept crossing each other's path. I was this guy known for just being a ladies' man, and he was known for being the baddest rapper kid coming up. We kept hearing about each other.

RYAN D ROLLINS I'm a military brat. My dad was in the air force and we moved to Marin County. There's an air force base up there—Hamilton Air Force Base. I lived in Novato, which is like ten to fifteen minutes up the highway from Marin City. It was a whole different thing back then; it was still more segregated. The Marin City people had been there for generations from the war, with the shipyards. That's where they all kind of migrated from Louisiana and Texas and whatnot. Even though I lived in Novato on the air force base, I always had a connection because we all kind of went to the same churches. My mom was involved with the Concerned Parents of Marin, which was a Black organization. Everyone was always involved in the community.

I was all things hip-hop my whole life. Being a creative-and-outspoken-type person, whatever came out, I wanted to do—from break dancing to rapping. So I can remember I was writing raps in seventh grade. I remember first hearing [Afrika Bambaataa's] "Planet Rock." In high school, I dressed exactly like Run-DMC.

I got into some trouble. So I had left and moved to Florida for a while. I was always talking to my friends on the phone, and they was like, "There's a new guy in town named Tupac. You need to rap against him. Y'all should battle." I was the best rapper, supposedly. Every time I would talk to them, they were talking about Tupac.

About a year later, I'm on my way back. I'm at the bus stop in Marin City, and it's funny, I'm with my partner who was a beatboxer, and here comes Tupac walking down the hill with somebody else. We meet at the bus stop. "This Tupac. This Ryan D. Y'all need to rap against each other." He rapped a prewritten; I cut a freestyle. He busted out "The Case of the Misplaced Mic."* It was one of those things where once we finished rapping against each other, from then on we were partners, we were in a group.

*One of Tupac's earliest recorded songs, released in 2007 on the posthumous album *Beginnings: The Lost Tapes 1988–1991.*

KENDRICK WELLS I had this friend who kept telling me about this kid she was doing theater with and how great he was but how annoying he was at the same time. I had heard little flashes about him in the streets, but the first I'd heard was from her, about theater.

I started in the same theater program as him in Marin. I had always done theater, since I was in high school at Abraham Lincoln High School in San Francisco. I went to this high school in Mill Valley after we moved to Sausalito and I joined the Tamalpais High School theater company, which was called the Ensemble Theater Company, and a few years later, she was in it, and then she's telling me about this new kid, Tupac. She said he would just do these shows, and he would never go to rehearsal. He was always late, but then he'd walk to the stage and just kill it. Being a theater buff, I was interested. And then, I would hear about him on the streets; there's this rapper, and it's the same guy.

Finally, we met at a party in Novato. When we first saw each other, even before speaking, we hugged, like we knew each other. He had been hearing all kinds of things about me. I was the ex–drug dealer that was kind and had lots of ladies and did things a different way. There was no violence in my thing—and we were like two refreshing characters. After we met that night, it was just on.

BARBARA OWENS I've been in teaching since '68, but by the time I got to Tam it was 1978. I was establishing myself as an English teacher then. The community then was very intellectually and creatively vibrant. Very fresh. There were so many artists that trickled into our community, good and bad. We had our drug issues. No lie. But I don't want that to characterize the culture. The issues around equity and Black Lives Matter were very fresh then, sadly. Yeah. So we were a community that was in that conversation and was in that struggle. Marin City has a tremendous history, tremendous community, tremendous sense of a generational culture that were always present in our school.

For us professionally, we were always working with their thinking to help them develop their writing and reading and critical thinking skills organically. We were young then. The pedagogy was new. We were breaking ground with pedagogy. And Tupac was just ripe for it. Discussion was a major feature of our classes. We graded on oral expression—listening and speaking. That was as important as the reading and writing.

Now, mind you, I was a bitch about it. I mean, I pushed. I was there for my whole soul. But I didn't have to with that group. His class was in the afternoon. You don't know what kind of energy you're going to get, especially after lunch at Tam at that time. God only knows what they were smoking. Herding cats kind of comes to mind. But he had that ability to get people to think with him. He created that kind of vortex that every teacher hopes like hell is going to happen. You have one student with that kind of a light on, it's catchy. It's contagious. It's wonderful in a classroom year. Everybody's thinking goes up.

In that particular class, he was the only African American student I had. Then look at that face. *If* he was going to look at you, he was going to *look at you.* You knew what he was thinking or doing. He carried himself in a way that was unignorable. He posed questions. If you communicate anything about his intellect, know that he fed it.

Now, did I see all of his life? Noooo. I'm over here in white land. I didn't have much of his backstory.

RYAN D ROLLINS He was totally different from us because we're from California and he came from New York and Baltimore. When he first came, he called himself MC New York. Quiet as it's kept, I tell people a thousand times, I'm the one who told him to start using the name Tupac: "Just go by your name." I used to tell him that all the time. He wanted to be MC New York forever. He finally agreed to go by his name, but he had to use the 2 instead of spelling it out. I said, "Whatever. That's a good compromise."

He was obviously more talented than everybody else. People who were into rapping could see it. Otherwise, you wouldn't know because he was dirt-poor. He was *poor* poor. He only had like one outfit, and he only had like one pair of shoes and they stunk. Whenever he would come over to my partner Demetrius's house we would tell him to leave his shoes outside. But his talent was incredible. I wasn't as committed as he was; Tupac made me step my rap game up. I instantly thought he was better than whoever was the dopest rapper out at the time. I'm like, *Pac could beat Rakim up.*

He gradually started coming around to the California style of things, but his talent was always obvious. He was in drama. He'd write poetry. Stuff nobody I'd ever met was doing. But me and him clicked because I grew up in a Black Power household. First books I read were [Eldridge Cleaver's] *Soul on Ice* and [Elijah Muhammad's] *Message to the Blackman in America.* I had been up on all this stuff since elementary school. So cats used to call me the militant one. "Ryan D is super Black."

So when Pac came, we used to sit around and Afeni would talk and tell us stuff. She was going through things, obviously, but she was just so smart. So Pac and I connected on that level. That's why our rap group was the One Nation MCs and we had songs like "Panther Power."

KENDRICK WELLS He was true hip-hop, meaning he was battle raps, he was a metaphor-first, East Coast–first rapper, and then the cherry on top was him teaching you your history—even though you don't want to hear it. I think back and I'm like, *Man, what if we all had listened and unified and took the message at that point somewhere else?* We were like, *Shut the fuck up. Let's go chase these bitches. Fuck these police.* Just stupid kids.

Ryan D was his rap buddy and they had clashed

many times, but they actually got one of the early battle raps on tape. That's pretty much what rap was back then: before they would write songs about a topic, we'd have these groups of people together and they would go heads up, crew against crew, same crew against crew and sometimes different crews, but it was all love. You were sharpening your skills. You were seeing who was the hottest. And Tupac was on the highest level. There were a couple people who would hit him every once in a while, like Ryan D or a few others, but he would hit back.

He came to Marin City and he woke everybody up. Everybody was rapping but everybody was still trying to make their money, still trying to do their side things, still trying to exist. He was like, *It's rap. It's all rap or nothing. We get up, we rehearse, we do this.* He got in with One Nation MCs and they brought him in like family.

RYAN D ROLLINS The group was me, Tupac, Demetrius, Gable, and Cousin Jay. That was the One Nation MCs. Cousin Jay because he had a car. Gable because he was a DJ and we liked his beats, but Demetrius had the equipment. We came up with the name listening to [Funkadelic's] "One Nation Under a Groove." I had rap books just like he had rap books. That's another way we connected: I looked at his rap books, and he looked at mine. But then when I'm looking at his rap books, he has poems in between his raps and shit. The way he wrote was different from the way I wrote: I wrote, like, full paragraphs with commas, and he just wrote line-for-line on the page. I was really fascinated by that, the way he wrote. It was so easy to read to rap it. He was way ahead of his time as a writer. Pac used to tell me, "You gotta write. The more you write, the better rapper you are."

*The Roland TR-808 is
a drum machine first
popularized in the
1980s. The E-mu SP-
1200 was a sampler
used in most early hip-
hop production.

Initially, it was just me, Gable, and Tupac at my house in Novato. I had an 808. I had a four-track. Gable had the two 1200s.* "Fantasy" was our first song. It was about a dream. Then we did "Never Be Beat." We did them on the 808 with Gable scratching. We were way better than everybody else around already. Just being able to record on the four-track like that. We really became a group after those two songs. Then we started hooking up with Demetrius at his house, because he just had all the records to mix. That's how we did "Panther Power," because that's like a Malcolm X speech and a James Brown drum scratch. We had a song called "One Nation MCs." That was our battle song. When we did that one at a party, the whole crowd had us feeling like superstars. I'll come in first, and I'm good. And then Tupac comes in, and he's mesmerizing. He's got a New York accent and sounds a little different. So we were unstoppable.

We did house parties. We did some shows, too. We opened for Def Jef. They were hating on us. They hated Tupac so bad. They wouldn't want to listen to our demos. We did shows with Mac Dre at the San Jose fairgrounds. We were at Oakland at the Festival at the Lake and we rapped against Oakland's Most Wanted, and they were a whole crew of gangsta gangstas. We did "One Nation MCs" and they gave us dap. We walked away holding our breath because they were like one hundred deep.

KENDRICK WELLS They were all living together in an apartment—Ryan D, Gable, all those guys.

RYAN D ROLLINS At one point, we all kind of stayed in the same apartment together. It was me, Demetrius, Tupac, and my partner Terry T from Louisiana.

KENDRICK WELLS Tupac was the greatest rapper on the planet, but he was a better cook than he was a rapper. I had Hamburger Helper on my shelf, butter and ketchup to make my own barbecue sauce, and some chicken breast in the fridge. So he was like, "Man, take me to the store." I take him, and I buy all of this shit he's telling me to buy. I've seen my mom cook this shit before, but he had all these techniques. He was so good you could tell he cooked for his mom and his sister. He put love into it. He taught me how to fry chicken. People love my chicken now because of him.

After he got famous, we'd be at his house and he had the Outlawz, so he'd cook whole meals. He'd cook gumbo. He'd cook soft-shell crab. He loved seafood. His mom would be sitting there—where his mom could get up and cook, too, she would sit down and say, "No, let the master do it."

RYAN D ROLLINS One time when we were living together, Tupac had cooked. And Terry had his new girlfriend. He said, "Tupac, man, clean all the fucking dishes you left in the kitchen." Tupac was lazy. Terry said, "You better have all those dishes cleaned by the time I get back," because he was going to cook that night. He left and we ended up playing fucking Tecmo Super Bowl and Nintendo all day long.

Hours passed, and here comes Terry: "Nigga, you didn't clean that kitchen yet!" Tupac said, "Fuck Terry, I ain't cleaning that kitchen." We were like, Aw, shit, this is gonna be good. Terry was a really aggressive person. Tupac wasn't a punk, but he couldn't fight at the time.

Tupac jumped up and ran over there. The rest of us were sitting by the couch. Tupac did the right thing and swung first. But he missed it. He swung hella hard.

He swung from fucking Kentucky. He missed with his hay-maker and hit the corner of the washing machine with his fist. We knew his hand was fucked up instantly because of the sound it made. Terry picked him up, slammed him on his back, and got to whooping on him. We had to break it up.

The funny thing about that story is we always said that Tupac hit that washing machine so hard that if he would've hit Terry he would've had a chance. His fist swole up. It was fucked up for a year—probably broken. We didn't have medical coverage. But he jumped out and he was ready to fight. He wasn't scared.

KENDRICK WELLS At some point, he wanted more. There was a lot of jealousy issues that came up where people wanted to fight and he just wanted to rap. So that's when he moved on, and he met up with Leila.*

*Tupac's mentor Leila Steinberg, who set him on his professional path.

RYAN D ROLLINS A lot of people saw the potential in Tupac; that's how he ended up in Santa Rosa with Leila.

KENDRICK WELLS As kids from Marin, we snuck out and jumped to Santa Rosa and Petaluma every chance we could because the girls out there treated us better than anyone in Marin City did. They knew where we were coming from. Even the parents of the kids were like, "You can stay here." It was just a different vibe.

RYAN D ROLLINS That was one of the places that niggas from Marin City used to go to terrorize the parties and tear it up.

KENDRICK WELLS Leila ran the fairgrounds in Petaluma. She was organizing shows. She was the shit. She was a kind person but she was also very businesslike, and she handpicked a bunch of guys who were serious and brought the talent to her county. The labels and managers and production companies knew who she was because they dealt with her personally.

She had heard about Tupac—I guess she'd put her feelers out there—and Tupac had heard about her. He was hell-bent on meeting her. He finally found the connection and she was like, "Come on up." I think I dropped him off, and once he was up there, he didn't come back for a while, and they started creating Strictly Dope.*

*Tupac's group with Ray Luv.

RYAN D ROLLINS He lived mostly with Afeni, but once he went out to Santa Rosa, he didn't really come back. His mom was on drugs and he'd had some fights out there. Pac was kind of torn because me and him was hella tight still. I was doing my own thing. I had money because I was doing other things. I had a nice car and everything. So I wasn't that serious about rap.

KENDRICK WELLS Leila's very close friends with Atron Gregory.† Atron told her, "You ever got somebody to take seriously, let me know." So she's like, "I got one."

†Digital Underground's executive producer and Tupac's first manager.

She sent Tupac and Ray Luv up there together. But the powers that be will separate you.

RYAN D ROLLINS I remember going to Leila's apartment and she was all into the culture. She was really fascinated by Pac. She had other little rappers. She had some kind of program. That's how I met Ray Luv. He was younger and wanted to be like us.

KENDRICK WELLS They bought Ray Luv out for the price of a song, and he went from being this sweet, happy-go-lucky guy to someone who seemed to be angry. I don't blame him. He wrote the song that got them on. Tupac was the greatest writer in hip-hop history, but the song that got them on—"Trapped"—was written mostly by Ray Luv. So they had to buy him out, pay him off, and make him disappear. He ended up on Mac Dre's old label.

RYAN D ROLLINS I was working on an album. This is right before 51.50.* I was fuckin' with Kendrick's studio. Kendrick had a studio. We were in the county jail together. So we kind of hooked up like that. He wanted to produce music and he knew about me and Pac, so he said, "This is what we're gonna do when we get out." Kendrick just had money. So Kendrick brought all the stuff for a studio and said he wanted me and Gable to record there. We even took a class at the College of Marin on recording studios. We got an A because we presented our album for our project.

During this time, Tupac was doing his own thing. He was in Santa Rosa fucking with Ray Luv and Strictly Dope. Then, not long after, he was doing his solo album, and that's when he signed with Atron. We hooked up because I had to go do ninety days. And before that, it was like, I was going to record a song with Pac before I turned myself in.

So I picked him up and I took him to San Francisco to Kendrick's studio, which was at his grandma's house at the

*51.50 Illegally Insane was a Marin City rap group featuring the producer Klark Gable and the rappers Ryan D, Levy Love, and TAC.

time. We did a song to "Mary Jane" by Rick James, and in true Tupac fashion, he wrote his rap in fifteen minutes.

We talked about a couple other songs we were going to do, but I know, at one point, Tupac and I walked to the store to go buy whatever—40s and some blunts, or something—and we were talking walking back and, I'll never forget, he said, "You know, I was just thinking I might let my manager look over this. So, you know, I might have to sign some releases for these songs and sign a contract or something."

I never thought anything about rap business, but Tupac already was, which was smart.

KENDRICK WELLS My adage had always been once you met Tupac, you knew where he was going, and you were either going to help him get there or get in the way.

RYAN D ROLLINS When he went to Santa Rosa I was still rapping. Me and Gable were still making beats. That's when we were just about to become 51.50. Leila became 51.50's first manager. She was gonna manage us full-time, but then a lot of legal stuff went down. So it didn't happen. But she helped us, put us in a better position.

When Leila hooked Pac up with Atron Gregory, that's when we started going around Digital Underground. I remember he said, "I have to go audition for dude," and he went and rapped for Shock.* That was it. I guess after that, Atron just told Shock to bring him. He ended up going to Japan with those guys not long after.

PUDGEE THA PHAT BASTARD Stretch† is the reason I know Tupac. Before we met, I was just doing demos and

*Shock G, also known as "Humpty Hump," was the frontman for Digital Underground, the Oakland rap group that also included Money B.

†Queens, New York, rapper who joined Tupac's Thug Life group. In 1994, they released their only album. In 1995, Stretch was shot and killed at age twenty-seven.

battling people in front of the Skate Key roller rink, and trying to write for other people.

I started writing songs at about thirteen years old. I heard Roxanne Shante's "Roxanne's Revenge" because I was a heavy kid, and my mother kind of groomed me to be sarcastic in response to people, you know, making comments about my weight or my glasses at the time. I tell people they don't pay attention to the steps. That was one of the steps that made me the writer that I am today—witty repartee, quick to respond to anything. Then it turned to barbs and vicious one-liners. And that kind of nurtured the rapper in me.

I worked at a McDonald's to pay for demos when I was fourteen and Al B. Sure was my manager. I wrote for Ghetto Girlz, who made a response to Geto Boys' "Mind Playing Tricks on Me" called "My Man's Playing Tricks on Me." I don't really do spoofs, so I didn't write that song, but I wrote the majority of the album, with the exception of a song written by Diamond D and Stretch from Live Squad, which was a group brought out by [New York City VJ] Doctor Dré.

Then I remember one day, Diamond D said to me, "No one's ever going to help you get on because you're better than them." And that kind of turned into a tic for me. After that, I became this super-duper aggressive emcee because I felt like, *Yeah, no one's given me opportunities.*

I knew Gang Starr from the beginning. I've been in the room with Latifah her whole career. So people would ask me to ghostwrite, but no one would say, "You go be the rapper." Once Diamond illuminated that for me, I went on a different path.

Women have always been my heroes; they champion me and they just lift me up, seriously. A friend of mine, her name is Essence. She had a song on the *New Jack City* soundtrack, called "Lyrics 2 the Rhythm," and she was signed with Grandmaster Flash. She was like, "Flash has to hear you." I signed with him, we recorded in his studio in the projects in Harlem, but after a while, I wasn't feeling the progression that I was looking for. So he got me to write for Roxanne Shante, which was the cathartic full-circle moment. But something went off in my head and said I shouldn't be working with Grandmaster Flash because I'm not getting money with him. He nurtured my talent. He was dope. He recorded me. But I needed to see things manifest for me if I was going to make this a career.

I went back to writing and getting on mixtapes, and then DJ Clue and I met up and started doing mixtapes together. I'd already gotten with every DJ I could to make sure that the world heard my voice. My cousin Lenny S, who works at Def Jam as VP of A & R now, worked in the mailroom at the time, and he and my cousin Burt stole a whole bunch of adhesive paper and posted my logo all over it—I'm still unsigned at the time—and they plastered New York with it. So being that my logo is a caricature of me with the middle finger, I kind of started picking up. I knew I made it one day when I was standing at the train station and a police officer walked up to me and said, "Is this you?" and he had my sticker on his ticket book.

I started gaining a lot of momentum. My godsister called up Red Hot Lover Tone from the Trackmasters.* He was like, "I hear you rhyme; let me hear something." I said, "Are you sitting down?" Three weeks later, after three weeks of demos, we had a deal with Warner Bros.

*The producer duo Poke and Tone, who have worked with Jay-Z, 50 Cent, Will Smith, and Destiny's Child, among many others.

When I was cutting the demo for "Checkin' Out the Ave.," Stretch called me like, "Yo, my boy wants to meet you. He is in love with that song." I was like, *Yeah, whatever, it's nice to have people appreciate my art. He's just a dancer.* It's Pac. We meet in Atlanta. He runs up to me and hugs me. I have no idea who this kid is, but he's hugging me like I just saved his life. He's like, "Yo! This record!" And that immediately struck me as different. In New York, it's very hard, if they're not in your camp, for someone to give you any type of accolades or give you any praise. But here he was losing his mind, yelling and screaming about this record. We became tight.

That was 1991. I'm a Cancer. He's a Gemini. We're really close in the summer area. So our spirits were the same, except for the dark moments where you're pondering change or you're in crisis. He was exuberant. He was always excited, always overjoyed, always outspoken and convicted in what he thought, and that is what grounded us.

D-SHOT I was in a group called the Click—me, E-40, B-Legit, Suga-T. We were doing the independent thing and dominating the independent world at the time. I was at the forefront of breaking down the barriers for independent rap music, me and my uncle St. Charles.* He was in the music industry in the seventies. I got him to make the move back into the industry. He's still a reverend to this day.

Meanwhile, as the Click is doing our thing, Tupac is with Digital Underground doing his thing. As we started breaking ground, he started to recognize us. He came down for one of 40's videos—"Practice Lookin' Hard."

*St. Charles was the executive of Solar Music Group, a hip-hop company and record label that was a gateway for Bay Area rap. (Unrelated to SOLAR Records, referenced later.)

After that he came back down to hang with us at the studio while we worked on the Click album.

He was a very, very motivated individual. Very sharp, very hardheaded. Back then, we were young and we kept a strap on everywhere we went because of the way the city was and the way things were happening in the streets back then. You had to keep one with you. When we were in the studio, I said, "Pac, don't worry about nothing, man. I got you." I pull out mine, right? This fool pulls out two of 'em! "I got mine, too."

When you're on your upswing, and you're from the city that you from, you got to remember: they tried to throw Jesus Christ off a cliff when he went back to his city.

KENDRICK WELLS A couple of cats would flex up to him, sit him down, he'd come back and smack the shit out of them, and then they'd want to fight, and one, in fact, did. One guy chased him and started whooping him. And he actually got sick of that because that outcome would come a lot when he was independent, until he got a group around him.

He was super uncoordinated, he was terrible. When you see him run, he was awkward as shit. He couldn't play any sports. He was not physically that dude. He had no skills. I was amazed later on when I moved to Houston and people were telling me how they were on tour with him and he was whipping dudes' asses. I was amazed.

RYAN D ROLLINS He was touring with Digital Underground and I was driving him around. They were at one of those hotels where it's one way in and it's a big U. It was already five hundred people in the parking lot and

I had a Delta with a peanut-butter top. I had a loud-ass stereo and you could hang out the sunroof. We pulled into the middle and Pac was hanging out the roof. He wasn't even famous yet, but everybody just assumed. We were kicking it with Queen Latifah all night. Chuck D and Kid 'N Play were there. The Afros.* Queen Latifah was telling us a story about how she had to fire one of her dancers because he was telling everybody she was gay. The whole time she's telling us this story she has a cigarette in her mouth. We're playing basketball and she's got a hard dribble and she's busting threes like it's nothing. She was way better than us. Cool as shit.

*The Afros were a New York rap group developed by Jam Master Jay and DJ Hurricane whose lone album was 1990's *Kickin' Afrolistics.*

Me and Pac went into a room with a ton of people. We're at the front door and we just started rapping. We end up battling each other. Heavy D was in there, and it was a dope-ass battle. I ain't gonna say I won, but a lot of people say I did. We walked over to the Denny's, which was right outside the hotel. Chuck D and the S1Ws were in a booth. Kid 'N Play were in the next booth. They all loved Pac. I knew he had the potential, all this shit falling into place for him, but that night was when I knew he'd be a superstar.

He had already been on tour, he had come back, even as a backup dancer. While they were gone they did "Same Song."† That was his first big song. I remember he was hella juiced about that. But he just had something that people gravitated toward. He just seemed genuine. It didn't matter what crowd we were around. We used to be around some gangstas, and, you know, they liked Pac. It didn't ever seem fake.

†A 1990 song from Digital Underground's *This Is an EP Release* (also included on the *Nothing but Trouble* movie soundtrack), featuring a verse by Tupac.

KENDRICK WELLS I remember this one night. We'd just seen De La Soul and Def Jef perform. Both me and

Tupac are starstruck. He's covering it the best because he's a badass motherfucker confident about himself. But I'm like, "I just saw Plug One and Plug Two on MTV!" Because of Leila, we got to go hang out with them at the hotel. He starts rapping for them. He does "Panther Power" or one of those One Nation verses. If we had recorded that, you'd be like, "That shit was dope" right now, because you know who he is. But they were basically like, "We see this every day. Is it over yet? Can we smoke some weed now?" They were polite. I don't have nothing bad to say about them. But I do like to revel in the fact that he became Tupac. What the fuck were they listening for if they couldn't see it? He would've signed with any of 'em. They could've had him.

RYAN D ROLLINS I went with Pac everywhere. To Shock's house in Berkeley—the one that burned down, before it burned down. That's how I became so close to so many of those guys—because me and Pac would strike out in my car and go everywhere. When he was recording his first album at Starlight,* I took him to damn near every session. I was often the one driving Pac. He didn't have a car. So I was always with him at Starlight in Richmond for his first album.

*Starlight Sound, the Richmond, California, recording studio used by many notable Bay Area artists, including Digital Underground, Tony! Toni! Toné!, and En Vogue.

Shock was there a lot of the time. We have like one song where we did sort of freestyling in the studio to the "What You Won't Do for Love" beat before it became "Do for Love."† Money B was there. Shock was just sitting playing the piano. I didn't even know anyone was recording—I didn't know outtakes existed until I heard them on YouTube. We were just sitting there, rolling blunts and laughing, and Shock just started rapping.

†The second posthumously released single from Tupac, which sampled Bobby Caldwell's 1978 song.

I've seen all of Pac's raps in his rap books before he recorded the songs. He talked about the songs ahead of time. I used to examine his raps, because I liked looking at them. I'd clown him for his poems with hearts and eyeballs drawn around them. I remember when he wrote "The Rose That Grew from Concrete." He literally showed me that poem. He was proud of it. Even at nineteen, I realized the significance of it.

PUDGEE THA PHAT BASTARD It was more poems in the beginning, so when he rhymed it wasn't the precision of an MC. I'm from New York. So, you know, Kool G Rap is one of my huge influences. But when I first started hearing him rhyme, I thought, *This is why my song was so important to him—because he's of that spirit.*

ROB MARRIOTT Tupac was not the greatest rapper in the beginning. The thing that makes him become a great emcee is that he starts to embody all the principles that hip-hop is presenting at that point. It took some time before Tupac became Tupac. It was in his blood. He was clearly charismatic, he had the training, from going to creative schools, and having the Black Panther background there. He had all the ingredients, but it took a couple of iterations for him to figure out what he was.

RYAN D ROLLINS All his songs during *2Pacalypse Now*— I'd seen most of them on paper. If you're really into rapping, you envision the whole process. Pac was prepared. He wrote more than everyone else. When I'm out in the street hustling, he's back at the house writing a rap. That was his dream, and, you know, he wanted to get out. Crack was crazy in the early nineties.

JUSTIN TINSLEY He grew up in a family that was very, very well aware of the evils of society and what could happen if you basically piss off the power structure. His mother won her case in May 1971, which is crazy. That was a month before he was born. So he was cultivated in prison in a lot of ways. He understood that struggle. He grew up in the crack era of the eighties, Reaganomics, the economic depression—that, of course, as all these other things do, disproportionately affected Black people.

KENDRICK WELLS Over the years, as I would conflict with law enforcement, I would learn things to say. When I met Tupac, we got pulled over a few times. This moth-erfucker knew his rights. I used to have to tell everybody else in my car to shut the fuck up because they would be manipulated otherwise. Tupac was not a person you tell to shut up; he was the guy you say, "Get him, Pac!" They weren't shooting us so much in Marin County but they were punking us. So it became known to the point that the cops stopped pulling me over with him because it went from a place where they could bully us to they're trying to escape without these mental blows upside their heads. Tupac knew more about the law than they did. He always spoke up, he always said what he knew, and he was well versed on the law. When he jaywalked that day he did not realize that Oakland police are a little bit different.* They whooped his ass.

*In 1991, Tupac was attacked by Oakland police after being stopped for jaywalking. He filed a lawsuit against the department that was eventually settled for $43,000.

RYAN D ROLLINS I remember when he got beat up by the police, because I saw him like a week later. He was fucked up. He had to cut all of his hair off. That's the only reason he cut his hair off—because they had knotted his head up so bad that he had big bald spots right there. He said he was just crossing the street. But I know Tupac. We had many confrontations with the police. And Tupac goes bad on the police. He would always talk shit. So I know. If he was jaywalking and the police said something to him, he immediately went to one hundred.

KENDRICK WELLS He jaywalked, he said something smart to the police. And what we as young Black men are told is don't talk back. Just do what you're told. His whole aura was *No, don't do what you're told. Do what any other human has the right to do. You should have that same respect.* It went onto a national stage. On a local stage, if I'm at war with a cop, the cop can lie, the DA will back him, the judge will back the DA. On a national stage, there's a thing called the truth that kind of fucks over everybody. That's when these police forces cower.

ROB MARRIOTT There's Digital Underground's "Same Song," where we weren't really aware of his politics so much, he was just a charismatic figure. He wasn't the best rapper, but he knew his way around a mic and he's really starting to understand how to be a showman. Then he started having these interactions with the police and we got the straitjacket Tupac. That's when people really started to notice him. He's saying things that most people didn't have the courage to say. Is this guy crazy, or is he telling the truth?

KHALIL KAIN This is what happened to Tupac: There were plenty of folks who did not necessarily disagree with what he was saying. They just didn't like the way he was saying it. But he's nineteen. He's angry. He's not trying to format a polite conversation. He's looking at this as dire; you're looking at it as a political cycle. *Nah, I'm not fucking wit' y'all.* When you're mad, how do you deal with somebody telling you "Fuck you"?

ROB MARRIOTT He was born basically incarcerated and in a courtroom. His mother was defending herself while he was in the womb. This would lead to a lifelong confrontation with the court systems, the police forces, and the government. It's really, I think, a case of how the trauma that you're born into lingers. He's always been harassed by the police since he was a child. Literally, the FBI was trying to find Assata Shakur* and harassing his family. His first memories are against the police and against the FBI. So it's kind of natural that he would get into these confrontations, considering that.

*A former member of the Black Liberation Army, Assata Shakur (no relation) was a friend of Afeni and her husband, Mutulu Shakur. Often referred to as Tupac's godmother.

KENDRICK WELLS I think Oakland opened his eyes. When he said something through a camera, then it came out on a TV, then he saw the reaction with people, and it got back to him—there was this big-ass loop that made Tupac, Tupac. I think Tupac was born after that ass-whooping. There's a hard part of Tupac that was born after the character from the movie *Juice*. But the guy who knows how to speak to a camera to make that shit ring, I think he was born that night in Oakland.

CHUCK WALKER *He fought in court; he sort of took all the legal efforts he could. He wrote very moderately that he was doing this in the name of the king. Basically: "I'm using my rights to get rid of the bad authorities and to bring back justice." But in action, he was killing Spaniards, burning down estates, burning down these terrible textile mills where Indians were basically enslaved. On the ground, you see much more radical movement. He led an uprising that spread really quickly.*

IV

LEVY LEE SIMON A lot of people would make comments that he was a rapper that became an actor. No. Most people didn't know he was an actor first. Before he ever entered into the hip-hop world, he was an actor. So when he got these opportunities, I was not surprised that he excelled.

GOBI RAHIMI Since he was a trained actor from the Baltimore School for the Arts, he knew how to project. He knew how to use emotions. He knew how to articulate feelings visually. So he was a phenomenon. I've yet to work with anyone who is comfortable and able to deliver at 1,000 percent the way he did in front of the camera.

RICHARD PILCHER I only knew him at a particular point in space and time, but if you look at his movies, he's just someone that the camera loved. You can't always tell that, frankly, in a classroom. I've had students that I thought were quite good and they got on camera and they're just not electric; other students, you think, *Yeah, they're solid.* They get on camera and you go, *Holy cow.* There's just something about the camera that some actors relate to in a kind of magical way, and he was one of them.

I remember seeing him in *Juice* and I just went, *Oh my god.* He is unbelievable on the camera—the eyes, what you see going on inside, the subtlety. Major movie-star time. He really had a tremendous career ahead of him in film as an actor. Denzel Washington—that sort of potential.

LEVY LEE SIMON When he did *Juice*, I remember thinking to myself before seeing the movie, *He better be good, man!* Because he represented us, you know? I knew what talent he had. I was never surprised by what he delivered.

JAKI BROWN After I cast *Boyz n the Hood*, I didn't meet anymore for jobs. They'd just say, "We want you to do the movie." Two months after *Boyz n the Hood*, I got a call from Ernest Dickerson, whom I didn't know. He told me he'd been Spike Lee's DP, and that he was going to be director of a film called *Juice*. He asked me to work the movie, but I told him I needed to read the script first. They sent me the script. I said, "We're back with more boys in the hood—without being typecast." Because *New Jack City* was happening at the time, and that was much more intense and much more violent. I decided to do it. They put me on a plane within a week.

I'm now in New York working with two guys that have never produced a film ever: David Heyman, who went on to get the entire Harry Potter series, and Neal Moritz, who did all of the Fast & Furious franchise. Ernest's career didn't go how theirs did.

KHALIL KAIN David Heyman went on to executive produce the entire Harry Potter franchise. Neal Moritz did all the Fast & Furious movies and a whole bunch of other shit. This is what happened after *Juice—for them.*

JAKI BROWN Here I am, fresh off *Boyz n the Hood.* I'm in their office, we're talking about breaking down the script, which is what you do with a director. But now I've got two producers who are both green. I explained to them how it goes. I get into what the director wants. His vision for the film is what I'm trying to create. I said, "You guys happen to be the producers and you want to get on board, that's fine. But you have to be in unison about saying yes or no." Normally, what happens is, I have a director that I'm work-ing with, and we love somebody, and then we have a pro-ducer who doesn't. And if the director is strong enough or has enough of a name, they can get what they want, or the producer and the director are on board and the studio says no. I've had all that happen. In this particular incident, Neal and David were the final word.

KHALIL KAIN When I met Pac, I was twenty-seven. I was not a kid. I grew up in New York City. My family was pretty much broke the entire time. We grew up in a cool area, though—the East Village, Lower East Side, very diverse. It was the eighties, nineties; there was crime, but if you knew people, you were fine. And if you grew up in New York, you were used to it.

I never was that kid in school that wanted to be an actor or be on the big screen. I wasn't necessarily ambitious. I was always being put in some program or other for gifted kids, but I still came from the street. So I never really fit in with those programs. It wasn't something that I was really ever getting value out of. I was generally causing problems.

I went to Hunter College High School. It's a college prep public/private school—it's getting money from the state. But at the same time, you have to be recommended and then take a test to get in. So I was recommended by my principal because of my grades. It's only me and this Asian kid from my school got into Hunter. Turns out we had to go to summer school that summer after sixth grade, to get us ready to go to seventh grade.

Get there in September, beginning of seventh grade, and then all of a sudden I see all these kids that were not in summer school with us—all these white kids. Now I'm on some shit about why some of these kids went to Hunter elementary school so they just sort of matriculated in or whatever the fuck. Immediately my radar was up and I was talking shit. All the fucking Asian kids, and Black kids, and the Puerto Rican kids were the kids in summer school. So I asked: "Did they not take the same fucking test?" "Yes." So what's good?

I pretty much carried that attitude well into my twenties. So by the time I was twenty-seven, I was banging around. I'm in survival mode. I've done every fucking job possible. I'm popular and I'm kind of known around the city and the nightlife and whatever. I'm able to make moves and people already know who I am. But that was more from just kind of being that New York dude.

There was a club in the city called the Roxy back then. It was the spot for hip-hop right when it was the jumping-off point. Afrika Bambaataa, Zulu Nation, Red Alert—all these DJs are up in there, killing it. Rock Steady Crew, Grandmaster Flash and the Furious Five. I saw Madonna perform in there. It opened as a roller disco in 1980. I was the dude back then on skates. So I ended up being there and I knew the owners from all the other clubs, so I could kind of move around. I didn't know what I was going to do, but my name carried a little bit of weight in this town, and I understood the importance of that, the value of that.

When the opportunity came to do some acting, that was more like an opportunity to make some extra money. It wasn't something that I was looking at as, like, *This could be it for me*. That's the unfortunate attitude of many of my brothers and sisters. We're not socialized to think in those terms—*What's my career gonna be?* No, what's my hustle going to be? How am I gonna pay the rent this month? How am I gonna put money in my pocket? Am I gonna be able to get some new boots for the winter? That was kind of more where my head was at.

So I was put in a place through other people's enthusiasm. I think I booked like three national commercials back to back to back. The agency that I went through was very excited. They're the ones who suggested, "Would you be interested in auditioning for some legit work?" I said yes. Do I know what legit work is? No. I don't know what the fuck that means. I know what work means, and that's what I heard. So I was like, "Yeah, I'm down." I figured whatever comes, I can handle it.

That means auditioning for film and television—like actual roles, not commercials. *Oh.* I find this out. All of a sudden now I'm being sent in for movies. I don't know what I'm doing yet. I'm very green, but I'm also honest with myself. I can understand that I don't really feel like the response was good from that audition. So how am I going to adjust? It wasn't about me becoming a better actor. It's about not taking an L. I got better, the feedback started getting better. I started getting some callbacks. I got close on a couple of things.

Then *Juice* happened.

JAKI BROWN They said they saw the character of Bishop being a rapper. So I sent Humpty from Digital Underground the script. He said, no, he didn't want to do it. Treach from Naughty by Nature—he was a rapper. So I called Shakim Compere, who was co-partnered with Dana Owens [Queen Latifah], to find out if he'd come audition for me. I told Shakim I wouldn't even have anybody else come in the day he comes in—just bypass all that other stuff and go right in to the director and producer.

Treach comes in. I love this guy. I mean, he's so sweet. Under that whole hard rapper, whatever, this man-child. We spent about an hour of me coaching him, and I realized he's not getting any better. But I didn't want to let Treach go away feeling like I nixed him. So I told the guys I was bringing in Treach. He reads, and he's not right.

There was a day where the producers wanted me to stay and I told my staff to go home. We started at seven a.m. sometimes, and it was maybe three p.m. when we quit. I told them they could go, because I'd often stay until eight or nine p.m. Ernest, David, and Neal went out location scouting. Gerard Brown, who was Ernest Dickerson's writing partner, was in his office. This is back in the day before they had people do things on camera and videotape—there's no more pictures and résumés and hard copy [today]. I'm going through dozens and dozens of pictures and résumés and trying to find that look, and who comes bouncing into my office.

This guy says, "Hi, hi, idliketoauditionforBish—"

I said, "Calm down. What do you want to do?"

"I'd like to audition for Bishop."

I'm looking at him: he's a slight, literally underweight-looking kid.

"What's your name?"

"Tupac Shakur." He said he'd read the entire script and he'd loved it. "I can play Bishop."

I said, "I'll tell you what, I'm going to give you some sides, which is like five pages from the script. I want you to look at it."

He had memorized the script already.

I read him. He was amazing—*amazing*. He underplayed Bishop, he didn't yell and scream and do all that stuff. Bishop being such a nasty killer, horrible person to be screaming and yelling—Tupac figured out the best way to play it was going under. He had the intense quality, but he was perfect.

I went and got Gerard. I told him I wanted him to see somebody.

"Who?"

"I have an actor here that I think is right for Bishop."

He walked out, looked at Tupac in my office, and said, "Where is he?"

"He's that kid."

He started to laugh. I said, "No, no, save it. I'm bringing him in. He's going to read for you. I want you to see what I saw."

Gerard saw him read. He says, "Jaki, he's amazing. He's perfect."

I sent Tupac to this place that sold burgers to hang out. I told him that my director and producers would be back that afternoon and I wanted him to do a callback. The guys come back from location scouting. They went into their office—they shared an office—and I told them: "I think I have Bishop."

"Who?"

"He's that kid you passed."

Again, they're laughing. So I go out and I get Tupac. I read with him just as I read with everybody. I'm the casting director. He read. He read again. I sent him out, and they said, nearly in unison, "Can we tell him he has the job now?"

I brought him back in, they told him, and he grabbed me and hugged me and he's crying.

KHALIL KAIN It was an audition for a low-budget independent film. They've got a character breakdown. They showed Q and Raheem and Bishop and Steel. There was no delineation for the audition. They were looking for new talent. They wanted you to come in and read. They had us all reading all the characters.

It was a long process. Weeks and weeks of bringing us back. I think I came back five or six times before I booked the job. But at the same time, by the time they had the four guys to do the film, we were pretty well versed. So not only was it an audition process, it was also a rehearsal process. They were bringing us into the room together in twos and fours. *Read the scene. Switch characters. Read it again.* It was hectic. They definitely put us through our paces.

I think I had somewhat of an advantage because I was older and my level of patience is better. My level of poise is better. I don't have a problem with these adults telling you what to do. A lot of the young Black actors that they brought in were also green to taking direction and being able to make adjustments. They really weren't able to do that.

Pac knew what an audition was. They were bringing in cats off of a look, off of the sound of their voice, the way that they walked and talked. They don't know how to break down a script. They don't know how to make an adjustment during an audition. Some of these mother-fuckers can barely read. Pac knew how this was going to run. He knew how to start a scene, how to build it up to a crescendo and then end it correctly. How to put a button on it. He also wanted to be a movie star. He had a specific ambition. He had already recognized: *This is a role that could propel me right to where I want to be. I've got this album ready to go. If I had this plus that—oh, shit.* None of us knew that. Pac did, though. This is the perfect commercial to *2Pacalypse Now.*

During the audition process, he wasn't fucking around. Talk about purpose: knows what he wants and goes after it. And he doesn't give a fuck about none of us, wasn't impressed by nobody. I'm looking at this kid over here, and he's flying on confidence. And his steps were correct. Like, he killed that last scene. I'm like, *Oh, shit, all right.* If you're smart, you take a look at your environment and you quickly pick out who you need to beat. *I want to win today; I need to beat this cat right here.* And that's what happened when we were in the room: I immediately iden-tified Pac as the cat to beat. This is the dude that's killing right now. So if I'm gonna get a job, I'm gonna have to be as good or better than this motherfucker right here. Because he's looking around at us like, *Y'all better come on, because I'm murdering y'all right now.*

When you get a role in a movie, you don't know what it's going to be. We didn't know *Juice* was going to be a cult fucking hit and have the sort of relevance that it does—for hip-hop culture, for urban culture, for Black culture. I read the script. There was nothing profound about the script for *Juice*. It was an indie movie about this crew doing street shit. They weren't even a gang. They were just kids, just friends. What's so special about that? So coming on the set, I had no idea what it was going to be.

And, see, that's the difference between me and Pac. He understood. *I know what it's going to be because it's going to be what I make it.* I was taking direction. He was like, *Let me do my shit. Get out the way.* So they were like, "All right, Pac, what do you want to do?" And he'd kill it. And they're like, "Okay, yeah, do that! That, that, that."

To have a young Black man like that, only eighteen years old, confident in his ability, not believing what white society is telling him about himself, believing in his own spirit—that is fucking monumental.

JAKI BROWN I had to find out what his background was because he'd been working with Humpty and I didn't know what he was doing. We're in the middle of casting, and we don't have a budget set for how much I'm paying everybody. There's only so much I could pay. Normally it's a minimum; at that time, let's say weekly might have been $1,000, might be up to $3,000. So now we're all cast. I've done the deal, except having done Tupac's deal. For whatever reason, he got a lot of money. I don't remember why, but you guys want him, he's worth every penny. I think he made $15,000.

KENDRICK WELLS After he cashed his *Juice* check, he got a little money. They paid him like fifteen grand—a check for $9,000 and a check for $6,000. I remember seeing the checks. He took the money and bought a silver collection, or maybe it was gold. Someone ripped him off in Oakland at gunpoint. He got robbed a few times. People were with him, and he thought those people were just going to make it not happen. And after this time, he was like, *This is never happening again.* Only person that he trusted to protect him was him. So he started buying guns. You go over and visit him and he'd show those guns off. I'm like, *What the . . . ? I don't care about guns. Show me a bad bitch!* In his mind, guns were going to stop people from taking advantage of him.

KHALIL KAIN Pac wanted to share his prosperity, to share his upward mobility, to share his ambition with young Black males that did not understand that this was something that they already possessed. He would invite anybody into his trailer to let them know: *Look at what I got. You can have this. This is not out of your reach.* One guy went in there and stole some jewelry, some pieces, and Pac whooped his ass. I brought this chick up to the set to show off. I wasn't even going to work that day. I just brought her up to the set to show her around and let her know that I'm a movie star and shit. I brought her up there, we round the corner up the street, and Big Stretch and Pac are fucking this kid up, like stomping him out. My girl Liz thought it was the movie, like they were shooting a scene or something. I was like, "That's not part of the movie."

We had a great time on the job otherwise. We played, we fought, we worked. We dug in. Everybody was fully committed. Ernest Dickerson is a marvelous human being. He helped create a safe environment for us. We didn't feel like we were being taken advantage of. We didn't feel like we were being overworked, underpaid, thrown around.

Pac and I had a fight on set over a blanket because it was a cold day. It was some really petty, childish shit. We were walking up the street. It was a wide shot. It was setting up the shot. It was cold outside. They had blankets and they got ready to shoot. They called ready, they would take the blankets from us, then action. They called ready, took the blanket from me; Pac still has his blanket. He's not giving up his blanket.

I said something to the effect of, "Well, we can hurry up and go if Pac would give up his blanket, let's go."

And he turned and said, "Keep my fucking name out your mouth."

I was like, "Fuck you, I'll say what the fuck I want."

And he was like, "Yeah, aiight, how about I fuck you up?"

I'm like, "How about you do it?"

And now they're separating us. Meanwhile, we're just cold.

Now word's going around set that Pac almost beat up Khalil. No. Khalil is a grown-ass man.

I came to him, and I was like, "Yo, B, we can go right over here."

And he was like, "Man, shut the fuck up, it was my bad."

He's a high-character dude. Immediately said, "That was my bad, I shouldn't have even came at you like that," whatever.

Then there was the Raheem death scene. It's the last shot of the day. It's the middle of the fucking night, man. We're beat up. Now Ernest is marking his shot and Pac is like, "Yeah, yeah, yeah." There was a level of intensity that needed to be there that wasn't there. I do believe Pac had a certain amount of reservation spiritually about doing this. It's in the script, but fuck, man, like, why is he doing this? How is he doing this? What caused him to do it? I could see he was still trying to connect the dots.

So on the next take when they yelled action and we started wrestling, I picked him up and, like, body-slammed him into the garbage cans.

"Cut!" Because that's not what was supposed to happen.

Soon as they yelled "Cut," Pac jumped up. "You motherfucker. Aiight, cool."

I got a big smile on my face. I'm like, "Yeah."

"I can't wait to buss you now."

The whole level is at a ten. You can hear a pin drop on the set. We had to get it right because there was only a certain amount of hoodies that we had that we could use the blood pack with.

But we hugged after that scene. We knew it was fire.

Everybody was not ready for Tupac's energy. Everybody could not handle that energy. For a lot of people, it was way too much. He loved and appreciated being around people who could function in that bubble.

I love that about Tupac. He always kept it 100. He told you straight up. Like, "Don't act stupid. We will fight. Wass up, bro, we fucking tonight? Yo, you want to smoke?" And he would rhyme at the drop of a hat. He would have us rolling. He was fun to be around.

I feel like Pac was bipolar or something. In his own private moments, he would be very quiet and introspective, but he definitely felt like when he walked in the room people needed to know he was there. If he stepped in a space, he had to fill it with energy. But then you're depleted, and then you have to recharge again.

KENDRICK WELLS Pac invited me out to New York while he was shooting *Juice*. I got to hang out at his trailer and see all of his costars, and I saw the transition. I saw him become Bishop. He said in a *Details* magazine interview that once he did Bishop, part of Bishop was always with him. And it might not be that he created it from the movie. I think there was a part of him inside that created the character. Pac was never a villain or a mean person. His whole thing was: *You walk toward me, you're risking your life.* But he was never saying, "I'm out to get you." In the case of Notorious B.I.G.—sort of. He came at him lyrically. But he's always been more about how boss ballers do. He was never aggressive going forward. He's always just aggressive on defense.

MARK ANTHONY NEAL The thing that really stuck out more so than the music, even twenty-five years later, was his acting ability, particularly his role as Bishop in *Juice*.

That was the moment I recognized that this is somebody that we should pay more attention to. It was an undistilled depiction of Black existentialism. The genius of pulling it off. What we see in this kind of a deep underlying rage, and even self-hatred. For someone that age to be able to play that off as an actor, to tap into this energy at such a young age, is unbelievable.

CHUCK WALKER *He tried to take the city of Cusco, this now-huge tourist center, a beautiful city. He didn't. He came to the hills with thirty thousand indigenous fighters and probably didn't come down because he knew he'd have to slaughter a lot of Indian people whom the Spanish put on the front lines. The Spanish sent in troops from Lima, most of whom were probably Afro-Peruvian. The Spanish commanders would be Spaniards, and the fighters, a lot of them, dragged out of bars, lower-class folks, which is often Afro-Peruvian blood.*

STELLA NAIR *Túpac Amaru II was doing really wonderfully. The tides shifted when the Spanish got Pumacahua, a Royalist commander who later became a revolutionary himself, to lead the forces against him. And it's because Pumacahua realized Túpac Amaru was not going to want to kill other indigenous people. Pumacahua put all the indigenous people on the front lines. That really undid Túpac Amaru.*

V

LESLIE GERARD I was the second person hired at Interscope in 1989. I came with Tom Whalley. I was with Tom at Capitol Records originally. Once he got the offer from Interscope from Ted Field, once he got settled, he brought me over with him. Our first release was Gerardo.* There were literally maybe ten people working at Interscope in the early days. John McClain, an A & R from A&M [Records], came simultaneously with Tom and I. Jimmy Iovine came in like six to eight months after we started.

*Ecuadorian-American rapper sometimes referred to as the "Latin Elvis" whose 1990 single "Rico Suave" reached number 7 on the *Billboard* Hot 100.

My role at Capitol was strictly as Tom Whalley's assistant. Then once we got to Interscope, we were so small that everybody wore a lot of different hats. Not only did I help Tom as an assistant, I was also his project coordinator. I was a music supervisor for *Bill and Ted's Bogus Journey*. Tom's first signing was Primus. Then Tupac. Then 4 Non Blondes. Those three artists were found in the Bay Area.

MOE Z MD A friend of mine from Long Beach named Radio got signed to Interscope. Then all of a sudden, it was like, No Doubt, Rico Suave, Red Hot Chili Peppers, Marilyn Manson getting signed and coming up.

LESLIE GERARD Tupac had a manager named Atron Gregory at the time. Atron wanted to do a label deal, so he came to Tom Whalley with three artists. I can't remember the third but one of them was Tupac and one of them was Money B. When we were listening to the music and stuff, Tupac was in Digital Underground at the time, so we knew who he was. But we didn't hear any music from Tupac except for the stuff that he did with Digital Underground. When Tom signed Tupac, he didn't want all three of them. He actually just wanted Money B, but Money B signed with Hollywood Records. We wanted to be in business with Atron, so we said, "Well, let's talk about Tupac."

Tom and I went out to meet Tupac and Atron at the Daily Grill by the Burbank airport. Had a meeting with him, told them we'd sign him on the spot, and we did. He was definitely more reserved. He was certainly articulate and knew what he wanted to do and where he wanted to go and be. He talked a lot about his time at the performing arts school in Baltimore. Then he mentioned his mom a little bit. At that time, he wasn't in touch with his mother, but he talked about her and her background. We didn't have a lot of time with him—probably two hours—but he was charming and on point.

KEVIN HOSMANN There was this friend of mine, Guy Manganiello, who was working on Capitol Records, and he went over to Priority Records. When the FBI sent the letter to Priority Records about "Fuck tha Police,"* they sent it to him. He was just a promotions guy, but it was addressed to him. He says, "Hey, I got this band over here. It's really heating up. Would you like to do some freelance?" So I go over there, and it's N.W.A's *Straight Outta*

*In August 1989, Milt Ahlerich, then assistant director of the FBI Office of Public Affairs, sent a letter to Priority Records stating, "[R]ecordings such as the one from N.W.A are both discouraging and degrading to these brave, dedicated officers. . . . I wanted you to be aware of the FBI's position relative to this song and its message."

Compton. I went over there to talk to Eazy-E; it seemed as if Eazy-E was the one who is the main guy—he and his manager, Jerry Heller. Those two guys were the guys you talk to. All of these guys were like, "Whatever you want me to do, I don't care." They weren't jaded at the time. They're all first-timers. So they didn't know they could be assholes yet. It was the way that I could get in there, because I was the cheap guy. They gave it to the kid because no one else wanted it again. Rap wouldn't get sold on the radio. It was considered Black music. It's a white industry.

So I'm working on *Straight Outta Compton.* I'd never done a photo shoot before. Roland Young,* he taught something called conceptual art, conceptual design. I want to tell a story here. I don't want to just take your photograph and put it on a cover. My two ideas: one is that your music is so powerful, and this is gangsta. It's hard shit. You want to look street. This is how we're going to do it.

Do a little bit of homework: Please look at the first Eazy-E record and the jumpsuit that he's in. And then look at *Eazy-Duz-It,* the one where he just got out of the car and it's dark. I did that cover to retaliate against the nonsense of that jumpsuit. They weren't New York. They were not New York in any way. They were West Coast rap, and they wanted to look hard.

KARL KANI I was born in Costa Rica, and my family moved to the United States when I was three years old. My dad used to get his clothes made by a tailor, so that kind of gave me the idea of how to make my own clothing. After my family split apart, we moved to East New York. That's when fashion became real to me. I wanted to go outside and play with the kids, and they were more worried about

*A designer who started at Capitol Records in 1964 and later became creative director of A&M Records. He was responsible for hundreds of album covers—for artists such as Cat Stevens, Carole King, and the Carpenters—and the famous Sunset Strip billboard promoting the Beatles' *Abbey Road.*

what kind of clothing I had on. They actually made fun of my clothes that my mother bought for me. I realized in the inner city, in the hood, fashion is a big statement. I thought about my dad's tailor, and I decided I wanted to make an outfit. All the kids wanted to know where I got it from, and I didn't want them to know about my tailor. I told them, "If you want one, I'll make you one." Really, that is how streetwear started. I started making clothing for myself and my friends liked it, so I started making clothing for them, too.

In the late eighties and nineties, the vibe all over New York was like the movie *Paid in Full*. Everybody was selling drugs back then. It was almost like it was legal. Everybody had money. Money was flowing in inner cities. You had teenage millionaires driving Rolls-Royces in Harlem. I used to have all these drug dealer guys giving me money so I could make outfits for them.

The most important day, I was sitting in the park bragging to these girls about how I made this outfit for that guy. His name was Joe. They were like, "No, you didn't."

"Yes, I did."

They said, "Tell him to come over here." He comes over.

One goes, "Who made that outfit for you?"

He's like, "Karl did, why?"

She asks if she can see his jacket. She starts looking at it, and she says, "If Karl made it, how come his name ain't on it then?"

She was being a smart-ass but she was 100 percent right. I was making clothing but I wasn't thinking about branding. I wasn't thinking about putting my name on anything. So after she said that, I went home and I started thinking like, *Damn, what should I call my clothing brand?* Because before Karl Kani, there were none. Let's make that very clear. We started before FUBU, Phat Farm, Enyce. None of them were even around.

I was thinking about all the brands we were wearing back then: Tommy Hilfiger, Calvin Klein, Giorgio Armani, Donna Karan. Those are the brand names we're putting on our backs. I wanted to be like them. I wanted to name the brand after me. My dad had changed our last name to an American name at the time—Williams. "Karl Williams Jeans" just didn't have a good ring to it. "Can I?" was a question I used to ask myself. *Can I do this? Can I be successful?* I knew if I called myself that, then every day I'd have to answer that question: "Yes, I can." That's how the Karl Kani brand was established.

One of the guys that I was hustling with, his name was AZ. He's a friend of mine. He got caught, and he's supposed to go to jail. But instead of going to jail, he ended up moving to California—to Orange County with his brother. I hadn't spoken to him for about two years. Back then it was no cell phones and beepers. You had to catch someone at their home. So one day I was at home, he called and said I should come to California and do custom-made clothing out there. I said, "There's nothing but sand out there."

Then he sends me this Eazy-E cassette tape in the mail. I started bumping it. I was like, *Wow, this is crazy. I didn't know California got hip-hop artists out there.* So I told him, "Find out where all the Black people are. Where do they hang out? Where is the culture?" So he rolled around and he heard about Crenshaw Boulevard. Every

Sunday on Crenshaw, all the gangbangers used to come up in their low-rider cars and put on a car show. So we figured this is where we need to be: right in the middle of South Central. But we didn't know it was a ghetto. When you're in a bad neighborhood in LA, you don't know it because there are still palm trees. In Brooklyn, you see broken glass and torn-up buildings. Out here, it always feels like paradise. We opened our store on Crenshaw June 23, 1989, right in the middle of the hood. We thought, *Game on.*

KEVIN HOSMANN The *Straight Outta Compton* cover was done at the corner of Alameda and First in the parking lot of a Comet Cafe. I barely knew what was Los Angeles at the time. No one knew what the fuck they were doing. We were just doing it.

The other idea was that my wife at the time went to FIDM [Fashion Institute of Design & Merchandising]. And there was this shoeshine place that was in a garage that she passed every day. "I want to do a shoeshine shot and I want you all to be up there. And you're, like, waiting around because it's now your turn. The world has changed. It is your turn. You've been waiting too long." I had a two-year-old daughter, blonde girl. I was going to put her in overalls, dirty up her face, and she was going to be this dirty white girl eating watermelon—role reversal with these Black kids who are just about to get their shoeshine because they were now in power. She was so petrified of these guys that she couldn't stay in that shot. So I had to get in that shot and shine Eazy-E's shoes. When I was explaining the concept to them, they all looked at each other like, *You're the craziest fuck we have ever met in our life. You're going to get us in trouble.* "No, no, no, we're going to sell some records because the image has to identify you as a power player and give the West Coast rap a look."

If you look at the first N.W.A record [*N.W.A. and the Posse*], they're actually on a loading dock and they have so many people around them. It's, like, well, who are the ones that are actually doing anything? How many people are in the group? So it's, like, no focus on who these people are. So we did the shoeshine shot and we made it black and white. And I think the only reason that didn't become the *Straight Outta Compton* cover is because it was like, *You put a fucking gun on the cover? I can't fit that into those places. They're not gonna sell this.* Because it was already offensive—the music was already offensive. If you look at the original cover and stuff like that, it doesn't have the original PMRC* logo yet. That was designed later. It wasn't even a badge. It was like, fuck them for having us have to put anything on the cover. And then what happens is you become the guy who did *Straight Outta Compton.* "We want you to do our cover."

That's why Tupac and Tom Whalley introduced themselves to me. He says, "Hey, do you have time to do a project? It's one of the guys from Digital Underground." I was trying to find a video and when I looked at a video, he was way in the back row. He was, again, like those N.W.A guys on that loading dock. When Ice Cube left N.W.A, I was doing his covers, and I was also doing N.W.A's *100 Miles and Runnin'.* At that time, they wanted to kill each other. Eazy-E had several houses in Compton, and I'd go over to one and they'd say, "Oh, you're working on Cube's stuff, too." And I go, "Yeah, actually I got some of

*The Parents Music Resource Center was a Washington, DC, group formed in 1985 by politicians' wives, including Tipper Gore, that successfully lobbied the recording industry to place warning stickers ("Parental Advisory: Explicit Lyrics") on albums containing potentially objectionable content.

his artwork in my car." They wanted me to bring in Cube's stuff so they could take a look at it. They were so envious of his leaving.

Tupac came into town, and I don't know why we were at Burbank Airport, but across the street from the airport itself was a restaurant called the Daily Grill. It was Tupac; a very attractive girlfriend; Tom Whalley; and Tom's assistant, Leslie Gerard. It was around noon and it was really just a place to meet because I don't think Interscope really had a place yet. That was my understanding. I've never seen that many rings on one human in my life. He was so blinged out. He just took the absolute direction from Tom Whalley from day one. It was one of those conversations where you knew he was something or people were promoting him. Whenever you have a band, at the very beginning, they're called sir, and everyone just kisses their ass. And as soon as their album tanks, then nobody returns their call. At that time, he was a golden boy. He was treated with kid gloves and Tom Whalley really gave him a lot of leash.

He never really seemed to captivate me—like, you're a brilliant guy, you're talented, I can see that you're going somewhere. He was just a good-looking kid. Obviously, he's one of the voices of all of rap and I just think the world of him now, but then they were shitting out rap artists by the dozen because of it starting to break. [Priority Records founder] Bryan Turner, who was a cheapskate, spent $0 on promotion for the Ice Cube album, and that record went number one the first week and sold a million within ten days. No promotion whatsoever. So they were just printing money.

We're at the Daily Grill. I go to the bathroom and I'm at the urinal and I hear, "That's where I've seen you!" I look and it's Tupac behind me. I go, "What?" "That's where I've seen you before: You're on that cover, aren't you? N.W.A." No one ever picked up on that. I thought it was the funniest thing that Tupac recognized me.

LESLIE GERARD We were all just a bunch of kids back then. We were just trying to make it happen, putting stuff out that we really liked. I don't think there was any really big game plan. When we met Atron, Tupac was just another artist that we were signing; nobody knew what he would represent later. We didn't even know what we had. I just looked at him and I said, *Wow, he's beautiful. Just a gorgeous, gorgeous man.* And then we just figured it out after that. A lot of people didn't know that he was an Interscope artist; they assume he was on Death Row. He was the only rap artist that we were directly working with. "Well, he's the artist. Let's see what he turns in, and we'll figure it out." That's kind of the way Tom worked. Not everybody worked like that, but Tom let the artist be the artist. He would just help them along the way to make them the best they could be.

ALEX ROBERTS Tupac was one of the kindest gentlemen I've ever met in my life. He was a kid when I first met him. I met him at the China Club just off Broadway. It was on the same side of the street as MTV and across the street from Sony BMG. I took my suit jacket off and I've got a black panther on my upper left arm. Tupac comes right over and goes, "Oh, that's a nice one. What do you know about the Panthers?" I go, "Probably not as much as you." And it started a conversation. He asked if I wanted a drink, I told him I was fine, and I went about my way.

The in-house lawyer for Sony BMG and I, we're sitting down speaking. He goes, "What do you think of Tupac?" I said, "I can't give you an answer. I've heard some of his earlier music. There's definitely something about him." Next thing I know, I look up and Pac's standing there with two drinks and he goes, "Oh, sorry, I didn't know you're with somebody. Sir, what are you drinking?" *Sir, what are you drinking?* To this in-house lawyer. So polite. I could tell immediately he was a very good person. Pac wore so many hats and he wore each one so naturally and to the best of his ability. I started to listen to some of *2Pacalypse Now*, and I wasn't a fan. But I liked his voice, and I knew it could be insane with the right producer.

SHARONDA DAVILA-IRVING I bought the first one—*2Pacalypse Now*. I was like, *This is so dope*. It was on a cassette tape and it was so super cool. Like, *Tupac can rap*. And it made sense to me that this is the kind of record it would be. I was really, really, really proud of him. But I was really scared for him. He's a Gemini. If a situation is getting hyped and escalated, a Gemini is right with it. And in my mind, at some point, we'll have the conversation.

The whole time, I felt like it was all of the things that he had shown me in that kitchen. The only thing that could potentially be shocking is the odds of people getting discovered. Was he going to be prepared to rock it out? Of course.

I think the political commentary, keeping the message of the people always within the midst of his conversation, is consistent with who he was raised to be. *There's no separation between who I am and how I carry the people with me.* That's just part of the DNA. Intelligence and political awareness, and leadership and service, were our pillars.

LESLIE GERARD Tupac was talking about writing about his life. One of the first songs that I heard from him was "Brenda's Got a Baby" and he wanted to go more down that road.

KENDRICK WELLS I saw him go into the bathroom with a cigarette and come out with "Brenda's Got a Baby." That wasn't rare. I think Tupac wrote a song every time he took a shit. Can't waste that time. But I remember this time he came running: "Check this out." And he was in it. The same nuances, the same rhythm that you eventually heard on the song. He was fitted. He had most of it finished but not all of it. He hadn't written the last verse yet. To me, it was just another Tupac song.

MARK ANTHONY NEAL My introduction to him was in his work with Digital Underground, as a dancer, and I very much remember the release of the first album, which was in part marketed as the solo album of a family member of Digital Underground; that was my initial context for him. At that time, I didn't have any real knowledge of his political lineage. I'm a New York guy. I had a real East Coast bias in terms of my taste in hip-hop. It was a moment where I was still very much invested in some of the work that was coming from folks like Public Enemy and KRS-One. The music didn't resonate with me initially. The song that did catch my ear of his early songs was "Brenda's Got a Baby." That struck me as something that was disruptive from what we were typically hearing from rappers at the time, especially male rappers.

PUDGEE THA PHAT BASTARD Not a lot of rappers were talking about socioeconomic things. But I did not like "Brenda's Got a Baby," and he knew it. I loved the message. I hated his rap style and how sad it was. "Trapped" was when I said, "Okay, you lit." But "Brenda" was not for me. I'm from New York. We're not like this. We're in the club. I loved "Same Song." He was killing it. That's part of why "Brenda" pissed me off. You do "Same Song" and you're rhyming with this ill, almost New York flow, and then come back with "Brenda's Got a Baby"? It was a disconnect for me.

KEVIN HOSMANN Victor Hall, who did a lot of photography up there for Digital Underground, was the guy who took those photographs for *2Pacalypse Now*. I didn't go up to the photo shoot, it was just done that way. Tupac came up with the hoods. I got back three images. I had nothing to work with. I have to step on this again—make it raw, dirty, more authentic or street. So this other guy named David Provost, he's credited on the cover for "photographic prints." He's actually a photographer that does really great black-and-white prints. I said, *Here's this image that I just hate, there's nothing to it. It's not working for me.* He basically just printed them oddly, so it's all that peppering and the color and all the weird sepia tone. Originally, that was a very clean image. The coloration and all of that is there because of that guy making it look a little bit more raw.

There's two no-nos on that cover. Tupac Shakur—his

name is not on that cover. He was a brand-new artist. You don't hide a brand-new artist by not having any knowledge of who the guy is. And then you never put a label or a title below the top third. If you're flipping through the bin, you need a quick read, so that the cover name and artist's name always had to be at the top third. But because of the time period—this was a time of the spaghetti box and CDs—I was able to put his name at the very bottom of it. And also the PMRC logo. Because what Bryan Turner told me is, that sells records. Put it big and bold. That logo sells more records than the guy's name.

KENDRICK WELLS I was a promoter. I would have these parties and all the kids in Marin would show up—like, thousands of kids. Some got in, some didn't. I rented this place on Howard Street. We tried to have a party there, and some chicks fought and the doors got kicked in. They shut down on us. But Tupac really liked the place because I was showing videos there, and he wanted to debut his video at his record release party for his first album, *2Pacalypse Now*. I believe it was "Trapped."

So Atron rented the place, but they told him that I couldn't come in there because their place had been trashed the last time I threw a party there. I believe Atron should have said, "Screw you. Do you want to rent it to me or not? Kendrick told us about this place." But basically everybody who was there when the fight broke out two months before was allowed to get in except for me.

Tupac told me to show up anyway. I get there and Atron throws me out. I'm outside for a little bit before Tupac snatches me up and brings me back in. When it's time to leave, me, Ryan D, Tupac, and a couple of guys get in this limo. He wants to go record over at this studio in Oakland. All of a sudden we hear gunfire—pop, pop, pop—we think people are shooting in the air, so we're, like, getting down. When we finally pull over at a gas station, there's bullet holes all on the side of the limo. We didn't know who that was or what that was about. I'm sure the limo driver had to explain what the fuck happened in his limo, but Pac was just like, "Pass the Hennessy," and we continued to the studio. It was never brought up again.

LESLIE GERARD He was always in the studio. It was always something new.

PUDGEE THA PHAT BASTARD When he was in New York City, he couldn't do much, right? Couldn't do many restaurants. So it was studios.

GOBI RAHIMI It was sort of like he let his hair down. He was really in his own space.

TIM NITZ I started getting interested in engineering, like back in my early twenties. Took a couple of classes and decided, *You know, I want to go ahead and try to make that a career.* I was a pretty good piano player, but then I just kept running into people that were better than me. I'm like, *What else can I do that is still related to the music industry?* So I went ahead and went to a recording school, and I just kept applying to studios in LA, all around town. There were way more big studios back then in, like, the late eighties. There was actually this thing called the Studio Menu. I would just go through that and I would just send out my résumé to like sixty studios.

I eventually got interviewed at Larrabee Studios and got hired as a runner. I worked for a couple years as a runner in a couple different studios around LA and I kind of got a lucky break. I started working at this place called Studio 56 as a runner and I kept sending my résumé out, and I sent one to this studio called Cherokee Studios. And they gave me an opportunity to become an assistant. A runner doesn't really go in the rooms, like not during sessions. Assistant engineers are, you know, now you're in the room; now you're in there working with the head engineer.

We were doing a lot of live recording, some mixing there. Then I kind of hopped around LA, working as an assistant at a couple different studios. When you're an assistant engineer, every once in a while you might get a little opportunity to engineer, if some client's got a really small budget; every once in a while you get thrown in the fire, but it was nothing ever really very permanent.

Then I started working in this studio called Sound Castle in Silver Lake. Most of the big studios in LA usually were two-room facilities with large SSL consoles, or in some cases, like a large Neve VR or something.* Sound Castle had two SSL rooms. It was kind of a more open studio.

*Solid State Logic and AMS Neve are British manufacturers of recording studio equipment.

A client came in for Capitol Records and the studio manager asked if I wanted to engineer for this client. So it's supposed to be a one-day thing. And then at the end of that day, the producer says, "Okay, well, we need a month here." I asked if they needed to get another engineer and he said, "We'll just use you."

The album was *19th Street LBC Compilation*. It was like a bunch of the guys from the Snoop Dogg clan. From there, I kept engineering mostly out of Sound Castle studios. Once you kind of become an independent engineer, you tend to go to a lot of studios. I worked with Bone Thugs-N-Harmony, LL Cool J, Snoop Dogg and Ice Cube and Dr. Dre.

This was kind of early for rap. This is the early nineties that we're talking about, and rap music wasn't quite pop music yet. It was still pretty much very genre specific. It didn't cross over to that degree yet. And it was just a lot of gangsta rap. So it didn't have the mass appeal.

A lot of the time, I was working with people, and I didn't know if they were— I mean, you knew who was a big artist, but I wasn't starstruck by any means working with any other rappers. There was a very similar vibe to all the sessions. Coming up as an engineer, there's a lot of, like, technical stuff that you learn—things about recording. Once I started working on rap sessions, that stuff got simplified dramatically. A lot of times they walk in with a drum machine, we plug in the drum machine, and that would be the song coming out of the drum machine, as opposed to there really being a lot of musicians in the room. We didn't use microphones that much. To me, it became sort of singular, sort of consistent—almost could have been the same artist every day for me. I'm really grateful because I got to make that transition.

Some Tupac stuff started coming in. I knew, *Okay, well, he's one of the bigger guys, kind of like Snoop*, but there was no differentiating factor. Obviously, he was still alive, so he didn't get the James Dean vibe to him yet.

The several times that I interacted with him, he was quiet. A producer would play a track and then play another track. Like, a producer would have to write a bunch of different tracks, right? And then the artists would go,

Yeah, let's do that one. So then, whatever track we settled on, we'd literally just loop the track.

In this one particular situation that I remember, it only took him about an hour to write the lyrics. He asked for a notepad and it seemed like he was starting from scratch to me.

COLIN WOLFE Tupac and I met at this studio in the Valley—I think the Valley Sound. I want to say '91, because I had just finished up the *Chronic* album. It hadn't come out yet, but we had just finished the production. I was working with MC Breed and he was there with intent to be a part of the project. We were together for about a week.

He had crazy, crazy energy, and he was mad cool. There wasn't a whole gang of people in the studio at the time. So there's nobody to impress, I guess. I think people are more themselves in situations like that. But he was always just a boisterous person—just loud, and just fun. He and MC Breed were great buddies. They were smoking a gang of weed and just having a good time. There was no threatening energy from him.

He would say, "Hit record," and you would keep that first take. There weren't any punches* or anything like that. Anything he laid down for the MC Breed album, all that stuff was his first take. Then he went back and doubled and tripled some stuff.

On "Gotta Get Mine," Pac and Breed are going back and forth because that was kind of like the concept song. But you can hear it because they're mixing up the lyrics. We kept that kind of stuff in because it was all in fun. Breed would have a title or concept for a song and then Tupac would riff off of that.

*A technique used in multitrack recordings to overwrite sounds.

On all the songs Tupac worked on, I came up with those tracks on the spot. I was staying at this house in Malibu that Dre was renting at the time because the house in Calabasas had caught fire. So insurance had rented this house in Malibu. So I was like, "Shit, I'm bored." So I asked Dre if I could go get the board that we had in the studio at the house and bring it to the beach house.

I went and got the board, wired it together, and was out there working on stuff. Warren G brought Tupac and DOC out there with him. DOC and MC Breed were really good friends. Warren G had a drum loop and this one guitar sample. I can't remember if they told me the concept already, but I just listened to what G had already and came up with that bass line, and then put the keyboards on there. It just came out of nowhere. It was the first thing I thought of. They say the first take is god's take.

PUDGEE THA PHAT BASTARD We got to the point where I understood that he does what he does. I was like, "Do you hear these ad libs? These doubles are off." He'd be like, "This sounds good to me. It don't gotta be perfect. I'm not perfect."

I'm somebody who wants clean vocals. I want everything to match. I want the double to be precision. For like three weeks after that, he didn't play me any songs. It went on forever. There are a couple of songs that I think Dre did, and I was like, *Thank god, somebody else was in the room.* But he loved to keep things natural and organic, which I didn't think was even a thing.

COLIN WOLFE We're back in Atlanta and I'm mixing *The New Breed*. Coming from N.W.A and being with Dre and all that, we mix our vocals a certain way. We did one single vocal and maybe one double track. We didn't even do a stereo double track. We did one and we'd either pan it to the right or to the left. So to me Pac sounded good, but from what Breed told me after the fact, he was upset that I didn't triple it.

I thought that with "Gotta Get Mine" it worked because Breed's vocals weren't tripled and doubled. I think it gave it continuity—them somewhat sounding the same, especially within going back and forth. I didn't even consider tripling it. Had I known it was part of his sound, maybe I would've. But you've got to understand that he wasn't even really Tupac yet. His first album had just come out. He was more with Digital Underground. So he was starting to get up there. But I wasn't even listening to a lot of other shit. We were working on the *Chronic* album. So I didn't know his sound per se.

TIM NITZ He definitely did, like, the double and triple thing. He would double and triple certain words for emphasis. Another rapper that would do that is Daz. But Pac definitely had it dialed in to kind of an art. It was very on point when he did it. He had a very good sense of timing and all that when he did it.

As far as what happened on the engineering side, he didn't seem to have either knowledge or interest about it. It was more, *You do your job, so I'm going to do my job. And if that happens, everything's good.* I kind of think it probably was something that someone introduced to him early on, and he was like, *Hey, this works. I like this; this works for me. I'm gonna keep doing it.*

Because of the nature of how music got produced in

the rap genre—since it was all mostly produced by drum machine—I remember, the first couple years I was working on it the sound quality was not good. It was like twelve-bit Linn 9000 or SP-12 drum machines. Especially with the East Coast stuff—they would use samples, and it didn't sound like they sampled it very well. By the time I got to working on the Tupac stuff, it was more clean and clear. And people had spent a couple years honing sounds—kick drum sounds and snare drum sounds. From a mixing standpoint, it wasn't hard to get it to sound good quickly, if you're an engineer that had decent ears. It wasn't a very long process. I don't remember the number of tracks in his songs being extensive at all.

In his sessions, he was never a "there to party" guy.

RYAN D ROLLINS Pac was always professional. When he got to the studio, he was usually ready to get in the booth. We always had fun going to the studio with Pac because it would be over quick.

MOE Z MD Pac was pleasant and high energy. He wanted to move and get stuff done fast. I noticed that from the first session because when we did "Outlaw," from *Me Against the World*, we did that in three hours. It was from me making the track to him dropping the lyrics, and doing a rough mix of it. That was unusual for me. I'm used to working with artists where it's like five in the morning and we got one song. If I left at five in the morning with Pac, he had done three songs with me, but also he would have two other studios in the complex booked with other producers in there and go back and forth. So he was gonna get him nine songs that night.

TIM NITZ I think I was working with a little side project he was trying to help promote, the Outlawz. He was in there for a little while, but he wasn't going to do a vocal or anything. He smoked and drank and ate some food. It was kind of like he was like, *Okay, here, I'm gonna bring the goods to have an enjoyable session with alcohol and weed and everything*. But I don't remember him being there the whole time.

MOE Z MD It wasn't like a bunch of females at the studio hanging out. He smoked his weed, but it was him and his brother, as opposed to a room full of people.

GOBI RAHIMI He was a workaholic. He would film a scene at night, we'd shoot a music video in the day, and if there was any time in between, he'd go to the studio. He was on a crazy schedule—a crazy self-imposed schedule, as if he knew what lay ahead. He was in a hurry to create a body of work that would outlast him.

TIM NITZ It always seemed like it was *Let's get the work done that we've got to get done*. The body of work that he has should make that obvious. He had hundreds of reels of tape of music.

LESLIE GERARD It felt like *2Pacalypse Now* was never going to be finished. Okay, we've got enough songs for this album, we can make another album. We release two albums in like thirteen months. When we were putting *Strictly* [*4 My N.I.G.G.A.Z...*] together, I was working with Eric on the designs.

ERIC ALTENBURGER My dad grew up at the end of World War II in Austria and was very adamant about what direction I was going to take in life. You can be a dentist, you could be an accountant—basically, jobs that would secure an income—this is what you need to do, whether you like it or not. I went to University of Delaware and made some friends who were taking all these art classes. I found it interesting. My father was like, "No, no, no, I'm not going to have my son be a starving artist." He didn't let me take any art classes. I got out of school and I had no interest in any of that other stuff. And I got a job doing board mechanicals at some small ad agency. And I was starving. No skills, no classes, no nothing. I was just sort of like learning on the fly. I was living on the Upper East Side in an apartment and this girl moved in. She happened to work for Atlantic Records. She worked in the art department under the art director. This was a time that was pre-computer, and they sent all of their board mechanicals out to this company, and the company charged astronomical numbers. She asked if I could do them. So she started feeding me mechanicals, and I was charging less than the company was, so I was getting a lot of work that way. Then slowly she started asking if I wanted to design, like, some PR CD that would go to radio stations. It wasn't for sale, so it's not like anybody was super worried about how it looked. They just didn't want to deal with it. Soon I was designing singles for sale and it kept getting a little bit bigger.

When Interscope came out, they had a distribution deal with Atlantic. They didn't have their own art department, so basically as part of the deal with Atlantic, whenever they signed an artist, the Atlantic art department would handle their artists. I was in Bob Efron's office when Tupac showed up in his lap. He was the creative director at Atlantic. He was a huge rock and roll guy. He was just like, "I don't understand this. I don't know what this is. I'm not relating to this. We're busy. You want to do this?" That was the first time I'd ever even heard of Tupac. That was my introduction to a whole other world. Doing comps and going over to this studio on Broadway and it's just dudes hanging out with milk crates full of albums just rolling blunts left and right. That was the first time I'd even heard of a blunt; that's how green and out of it I was. But here's Pac just flipping samples and I'm some white boy just watching it happen.

I think it was more or less, "Here's the song. Here's the cassette, listen to it, pick out some images, put it together." He wasn't getting much love, and a sense of, like, *Let's really put a lot of forethought into what we're putting out there. The imagery we're throwing out.* That was Atlantic. But Interscope was cool. They were pretty much like, "Do what you want." In our conversations, he wanted a destruction-type thing with burning buildings. He mentioned blue and red cop lights. It was carryover from *2Pacalypse Now.*

BLU The first thing that drew me to Pac was seeing commercials for *Juice* as a kid. I remember discovering him as an actor before I even knew he was a rapper. Then later, I saw the CD for *Strictly 4 My N.I.G.G.A.Z...* at my dad's house. And I remember putting that CD in when I was, I think, like nine or ten. I really didn't know what I was expecting. He looked like Superman to me on the album cover. He *is* hip-hop Superman.

KARL KANI We thought we were about to blow up, but the story didn't go that way. Some gangbangers ended up coming in and robbing our store at gunpoint; took all of our samples. We had a choice at that point: Should we stay in Los Angeles or go back to New York with our tail between our legs? We refused to do that.

Everything that happened to us happened organically. Hip-hop needed a clothing designer and Karl Kani needed the culture for his brand. It was always like a perfect marriage. They loved the fact they could relate to us. They loved the fact that we could fit them the right way. They love the fact that we're utilizing them in our advertisements. Back then, no other fashion designers even wanted hip-hop artists in their clothing.

Tupac used to wear my clothes all the time. Every time we open a magazine we see Tupac wearing it. Then we see him wearing it in the "Keep Ya Head Up" video. He has it on in the MC Breed video "Gotta Get Mine." He was religiously wearing the clothing. I knew I had to meet him.

AZ handled all the street stuff for us. I told him to get in touch with Tupac for me. Tupac happens to know a guy named Stretch from Queens, one of the guys from Thug Life who, later, got killed. Stretch gave us the number for the record company and they told us Tupac would be at the Hotel Nikko in Beverly Hills at this time and you can meet him there. It was 1993.

We got to the hotel. We go into the room and he's sitting at the table on a computer writing a script for a movie. He was talking to us and we had a very intelligent conversation. We're talking about hip-hop, Black culture, Black Panthers, and Tupac was smoking blunt after blunt.

But he was laser focused—multitasking, smoking blunts, typing, and still talking to me A1.

There was one issue: he never looked up at me. It was weirding me out, like, the guy would not look up and look at us. He's in a room by himself, no security. And I had something I was planning to ask him, but I don't want to ask if this guy isn't looking at me.

So finally, room service comes to the room and knocks on the door. I remember the room service guy put a towel over his face, there was so much weed smoke in the room. He was choking. I said, "Yo, Pac, how much would you charge me to do an ad?"

He got really quiet, and that's when he finally looked up. I thought I'd fucked up until he said, "Man, you Black. I don't charge my people for nothing."

My heart just stops for a second. I mean, this is Tupac we're talking about. He wasn't as big as he was going to get yet, but he was going places. This was right before *Above the Rim*.* He said, "I want one thing. Can you put Thug Life in some of the ads with me?" That's when the ice broke and the other Pac came out—the Gemini Pac.

He was like, "I've got this idea for you: I want to be sitting on this basketball rim in Harlem. No shirt on, just your Karl Kani boots on." He visually directed the whole photo shoot within seconds. He had it all in his mind.

Everything he said, he did. Two weeks later, we were in New York. We did the shoot. It was one of the most iconic campaigns we've ever done. Tupac didn't even want any free clothing. He said, "I want to pay for my clothing. You're a Black company. I'm gonna blow your shit up." No money was ever exchanged between us. Nothing. Pac was just a straight-up G.

*The 1994 film in which Tupac starred as Birdie, a vicious Harlem gangster who will stop at nothing to win a playground basketball tournament.

*In November 1993, Tupac was charged with shooting two off-duty police officers in Atlanta while there for a performance at Clark Atlanta University. Prosecutors later dropped the charges, believing Tupac had acted in self-defense.

JUSTIN TINSLEY *Strictly 4 My N.I.G.G.A.Z...* represents that last moment of complete clarity from Tupac before, obviously, the shooting in Atlanta* with the cops and of course the rape case later that year. I think *Strictly* is the most-Tupac Tupac that we could have ever gotten. It shows the Panther was in him, and you can see where he grew up in the streets with songs like "Holler If Ya Hear Me" and "The Streetz R Deathrow." But then you had the playboy Tupac, which is "I Get Around," and then "Keep Ya Head Up," which is another great example of, like, how, he was a Gemini's Gemini. He could make a song like "I Get Around," sexually promiscuous, but then two songs later be like, *Look, we gotta protect our women.* He was a Gemini—good, bad, and indifferent.

PUDGEE THA PHAT BASTARD Kanye is a Gemini; so is Trump. They're all the same creature, in a way.

ROB MARRIOTT I edited a story that dream hampton wrote for *The Source.* I was getting more details about the Atlanta incident and his mentality. I'd gone down to Atlanta for the cover shoot. He was remarkably on time and easy to work with. We got these great shots. And we went to his house afterward. As we rolled up to the house, we heard a gunshot. We're like, *What the hell is going on?* We got to the door and he greeted us with champagne bottles, and he was saying that he had so much pressure on him that he had to shoot the wall, just shoot a gun off because he's so stressed.

The first thing I noticed was, like, the level of awareness that he had all the time. He was very much a person in the present moment and he was constantly drawing information. And then not only drawing it, but being able to distill all the information that he had in such a clear way, even though his world was so chaotic. He was able to maintain this clarity of thought and a capacity for reason that was belied by the chaotic nature of his life. We walk through his house, he just shot a gun into the wall but greets us at the door with champagne bottles. And the first thing I noticed is the Nefertiti tattoo on his chest and him being able to articulate why he had this tattoo.

That was the experience of him: gunshots in the wall, and then really articulate expressions of his love for Black women.

LESLIE GERARD I went out on the road with Tupac. I was five months pregnant with my son, and it was me, Tupac, and Fade, who was our hip-hop promo guy. We went out on the road for six weeks breaking *Strictly*. We went into all of these kind of underground radio stations that were in people's homes and dorms, because hip-hop wasn't on the radio. It was pirate radio. We were trying to be true to his background and where he came from. We went to the school in Baltimore and he was able to do an assembly in the auditorium. One of the stops that we made was in Harlem, back in like '92. We'd just done this interview with some MTV hip-hop guy, and Tupac and his buddies couldn't get a cab. The cabs kept just rolling by. I had to hail the cab for him. That's how separate the worlds were. It was a lot of shaking hands and kissing babies at that point, and Pac couldn't have been more charming.

When Vice President Dan Quayle threatened Time Warner,* nobody cared. You know, we had Death Row

*In 1992, Dan Quayle called for *2Pacalypse Now* to be removed from stores when it was connected to the shooting of a state trooper in Texas.

Records on our label. So that didn't even scan in any meaningful way. That was like, *Whatever, dude.*

MARK ANTHONY NEAL When his music gets referenced in a shooting, it's a moment where the government, and C. Delores Tucker, and Bill Bennett,* and all these folks are going after Time Warner for gangsta rap, and Tupac is engulfed in that. I think for many Americans, Tupac is the guy some guy was listening to when he shot somebody. People realized that gangsta rap is being bought by a significant amount of young white kids. And white parents are losing their minds over this, and Tupac becomes a focal point, even more so than N.W.A, because at least with N.W.A you had a group. Tupac was a singular figure who also was very articulate about his choices—why he did what he did and why he said what he did—who also did have this longer legacy with the Black Panther Party. It was dangerous in a way that N.W.A could never be dangerous.

*A civil rights activist and a conservative Republican, respectively, who joined forces against gangsta rap. In a coauthored 1995 op-ed for the *New York Times*, they wrote, "We are not calling for censorship. We are both virtual absolutists on the First Amendment. Our appeal is to a sense of corporate responsibility and simple decency. There are things no one should sell . . . Corporations that peddle filth for profit are doing enormous damage to children. For the sake of children, they should stop now."

ROB MARRIOTT It wasn't enough to say, "Fuck the police." He literally got into confrontations with them. All of the elements that Tupac spoke about, he actually lived. That was part of his appeal.

CHUCK WALKER *Túpac Amaru II was captured in 1781 and then executed. Peruvians know the story of the execution the way Americans know the story of Washington crossing the Delaware. It was just terribly brutal. They tried to quarter him—pulling off his four limbs via horses; they actually got eight horses. They wouldn't come off. It's really hard to do. So they ended up cutting out his tongue and hanging him. Before that, he'd witnessed the execution of his wife, Micaela Bastidas, who was super important to the rebellion. So he, his wife, his son, and his inner circle get executed in a very bloody fashion.*

VI

WENDY DAY I started listening to rap in 1980, and I fell in love with the passion and the energy in the music. I was making quite a bit of money in corporate America at the time, which was very attractive to me, because I come from relatively lower-middle-class and humble beginnings. One of my life goals was to make money. The expression back then was "Whoever dies with the most toys wins," and I was playing to win. Then, in the early 1990s, as the wisdom of age started to set in, I realized that wasn't necessarily the most important thing in life, and for me, helping others took precedence.

In 1992, I started Rap Coalition, which is a not-for-profit organization that helps artists get out of bad deals when they're signed to a major label. For example, a label shelves them, or they're signed to a management agreement or production agreement with somebody that's not doing the job that they're supposed to be doing. That's the reactive part of what we do. The proactive side is we offer a lot of educational resources to help artists understand the music business as a whole, how the industry works, and also help them choose a team—meaning how to choose an attorney, a manager, an accountant. Basically, how to succeed in music, or how to make money in music.

From Rap Coalition, I was able to start a for-profit called Power Moves, which is how I was able to fund Rap Coalition and still do to this day. Power Moves is the company that helps artists get into good deals; we negotiate for artists that have leverage. This was right around the time that I met Tupac.

ETHAN BROWN New York from '90 to '94. Giuliani comes in then and everything totally changes. But the nightlife before then is fascinating. There's such a mix of people. It's almost impossible to imagine now. You have gangsters, Wall Street guys, LGBT people, everybody kind of mixed into this world. And there's a lot of underworld stuff running through these clubs. Peter Gatien would have this Sunday-night party with Funkmaster Flex.* It was basically the most important club event in the history of hip-hop.

*Tunnel Sundays was hosted at the eponymous Chelsea neighborhood nightclub from 1992 until the club closed in 2001.

TERRENCE "KLEPT" HARDING I grew up in Brooklyn. I was always in the streets. I was a hustler, not a drug dealer. But I used to get a lot of money in the early nineties.

I met Big in 1994. I always wanted to get on and rap; I was doing demos, and I'd start rapping and I'd stop. The night of the Grammys, I was sick as a dog. I was staying home and all my boys, they were like, "Yo, yo, let's go to the Tunnel, let's go to the Tunnel, it's going to be the Grammy after-party." Somebody convinced me to go. Nowadays people spend thousands of dollars on weed, but back in those days, people used to buy a dime bag or two and just chill. I didn't like to smoke when I was sick. We went to the weed spot on Nostrand and Sterling, which was the go-to spot for skunk weed; got a dime bag; and then we all drove to the Tunnel. We all had cars. I told my boys I was smoking the weed with the person that was putting me on that night, because I went there with intentions to get on in rap.

Everybody was there. Wu-Tang had just had "C.R.E.A.M." I'm seeing all these different artists. I'm sitting down in the corner like, *I gotta figure out who I want to rap to*, but I'm beat, like I have a severe flu, like, some fucked-up shit. I did that for so long, the next thing that happened was the lights came on and the party was over. I jumped up and freaked out. I'm like, *Oh shit*. I'm looking for anybody. I'm ready to rap to the bartender. If you haven't been in the Tunnel, the bar is long, so I'm walking around the bar to look and see who I can catch because once the lights come on, it's over. As I'm walking toward the door to lead to the big vestibule area of the Tunnel—people getting their coats or whatever and all that—I see Big standing up. I'm like, *Oh shit, there go Biggie Smalls. That's an ill nigga*, thinking I'm going to step to him, in my mind.

So I walk up to Big and I say, "Yo, you know my man June in Brooklyn. My name is Klept. I'm the nicest nigga that ain't out." Looked him right in the face.

He looked at me and paused for a second, then stuck his hand out and said, "Yo, I believe you."

I don't think he really believed me when he said it, but he did it in a genuine way. All he had then was "Party and Bullshit" and [guest vocals on Mary J. Blige's remix album of] *What's the 411?* He had a crazy buzz, but he didn't have anything out yet. Me, as a rapper, I knew he was an ill nigga. I was that fashion dude—I had DKNY jewelry, mad Polo shit—that's my history in the streets.

In the midst of him saying, "Yo, I believe you," he's

standing around with some dudes who turn out to be Bönz Malone, Lil' Cease, and Chico Del Vec. I didn't know who Lil' Cease and Chico Del Vec were. In the interim—remember, this is when Big was just coming up, so he wasn't in the making-money stages yet—he goes, "Yo, Cease, we gonna go get some breakfast? Yo, let's go get a taxi."

I'm like, "Y'all trying to go somewhere? I got a car." I told them I'd meet them out front. In my mind, I already knew what time it was: I'm like, *This motherfucker don't know that I just bought a brand-new Q45, fresh out the box.* The Tunnel was on Twenty-Seventh Street, so when the party was over, traffic was moving slowly up the block. As I pulled up to the front of the Tunnel, and Big and them looked over and saw what I was in, that spaceship, their eyes looked like kids seeing Santa Claus. They looked like, *Oh shit, this motherfucker doing his thing, whoever the fuck he is.*

Now we're posted up right in the front of the Tunnel when everybody is coming out. So everybody's seein' the car, and seein' Big in the passenger seat. Big was like, "We're going to go to Chelsea [Square] Diner," which was the twenty-four-hour after-club spot in Manhattan. He bought everybody breakfast.

After, we got in my car, and I rolled up the bag of weed. I had the Souls of Mischief's "Never No More" on cassette because I liked that beat, and I rapped every lyric I had. Big said, "Take my number, let's connect tomorrow."

From that day forward, me and Big, we would be like the Dynamic Duo going on through New York. When he rapped "Q45 by my side," he was talking about mine. He just stuck to me because I had the style and swag. He had the lyrics and the presence. We used to go pick up Nas in

Queens. This is when they were all coming up. They really had no money yet. I was taking bread—hence the name Klept.

ETHAN BROWN Gatien's clubs were at their peak.* And that's when Pac was there.

WENDY DAY I remember being on line at a club called the Palladium on Fourteenth Street, and I remember him being behind me and he was there with his entourage and they were very loud and shouting at passersby. They were catcalling females as they walked by and being obnoxious. I remember going to the back of the line, just so I wouldn't have to be standing next to them. It was my first introduction to the world of Tupac.

KARL KANI My conversations with Tupac after he got super famous were very different. He was a different person at the time. It was strange.

PUDGEE THA PHAT BASTARD I've always felt like hangers—we call them the strays—but the hangers-on will come out of nowhere. Makeup artists, DJs, other rappers—everybody wants to become your best friend when you're high-profile.

RICHARD PILCHER What happened to him in terms of his being commercialized, and the persona he adopted, still boggles my mind. I understand what happens to someone in that situation. But I . . . You know, he came back to school a couple of times when he was starting to get famous. And at least the second time he came back, he was

*In addition to the Tunnel, Gatien's portfolio of Manhattan clubs included the Limelight and the Palladium.

sort of with his posse and it was like, they were defending him. I remember he said to me at one point, "It is so weird that I walk in a room and all these middle-aged white men in suits run over to me and ask me what I need."

The things that were all of a sudden available to this young man who'd been raised in poverty, and what that does to your brain, I don't know. Because I've never been anywhere close to that. But it has to be really tough to deal with. So what happened to him—the kind of persona that he adopted, or maybe had to adopt, or was encouraged to adopt—being a tough thug and no one to mess with and all of that sort of thing, it just didn't jibe with the kid I knew.

D-SHOT If he would have stayed away from the gang-bangers and stayed connected with his real cats from the Bay, he wouldn't have gotten caught up in all that.

KENDRICK WELLS I was a fan of Tupac, the dude, the cool motherfucker who'd party with me. We messed with girls together and had fun together. I was happy with his career rising. But I wasn't a friend because of his music. Music was second to me. Him reaching his potential was very important to me, but the music was second. I wasn't a fan yet. I wasn't a fan until the *Me Against the World* album.

MOE Z MD That was one of the weirdest records I ever worked on—*Me Against the World*. I've never done a record like that. That was so weird.

Dre was still on Ruthless [Records] when I was hanging out with him. He was trying to get me to be a part of N.W.A because Ice Cube had left. I couldn't really move

the way that they moved. I just . . . I had a different thing.
I wasn't a gangster. I didn't want to be around that atmo-
sphere, which made it hard because I grew up with Snoop
and Warren G and all those guys. And they were wanting
to do music with me, but I knew that they did street stuff
that I wasn't really into. By this time, I had gotten signed,
got a publishing deal and a manager, and now I'm doing
pop songs. I'm doing songs for kids on Capitol Records,
A&M, but under another producer. He was supposed to
be grooming us, but after about six years doing that pop
music, I was kind of getting fed up, because this guy was
getting all the credit. One of the songs that I wrote myself,
he ended up being the producer of it, and they cut me out
of the deal. So I needed to do something else.

I was doing stuff at Interscope for Radio and being
up there all the time. They started to lose interest in Radio,
not giving him as much attention. I was just sitting at the
crib and still playing at church, you know, every Sunday,
and then all of a sudden, Tupac called Radio's manager
and was hyped about me and wanted me to do some remixes for him to see how I would work with him. He said
to send him some tracks, too.

I made a cassette with some tracks on it, and they
mailed it to him. It was on a Wednesday. They mailed
it to him. He got it on Friday. He loved it. I think I went
to the studio on that Thursday and did "Cradle to the
Grave," "Runnin' [from the Police]" with Biggie, and "Lord
Knows." So he heard those and was like, "Oh my god,"
and flew me to New York on that Monday to work on another song with him. It was "Outlaw," and we worked out
of Quad Studios.

Interscope was notorious for reworking songs. He

would do a song to one track. And then they would get another producer in to get what they called a remix. If they liked that better, they used that version. He wanted to try to get the best stuff with the music that he chose. I was one of the ones that could give him that. With the energy that we had together, we created a different kind of vibe. It was kind of a mixture of *The Chronic* and what Ice Cube did on his first album with hip-hoppish beats with samples but also keeping it funky. I added my little twists and turns but that's the energy that we're trying to have. I think the label was trying to steer it a different way. They had other producers using my elements and the vibe that I had going on with my thing.

I sat in on some of the other sessions and they were cool because I was getting to meet some of the other producers. I met the two white guys that did "Me Against the World." I just sat in for a while and listened. And they asked if I could offer anything, and I didn't really have anything; they kind of seemed like they had it together. I sat in on "If I Die 2Nite" after it was done. My engineer was mixing it. And I came in there just to sit around, to hang out. Pac sampled me saying, "Tonight's the night I get in some shit."

It still was a tough road for me. Some of my stuff got changed. In fact, "Lord Knows" is a mixture of three different versions: the original guy, Brian G; some elements from my remix; and some elements from Tony Pizarro's remix. And the label had my engineer piece it together.

Creating it with him was great and fun, but all of the records I did on there, they went back and did an extra mix that I wasn't there for. And some of them I'm not happy with. But it still turned out to be a great album.

EZI CUT Soulshock, Jay-B, and me* had a few sessions spaced out in the Valley. They rented a house in Encino. We basically just had a few late-night sessions [with] an old sampler, some old-school equipment. We were just vibing and cooking up, the three of us. And I remember we probably came out with two demos. One of them was the "Old School" demo track. We kind of left it alone. Didn't give it much thought. A month or two later, Jay-B and I had gotten our asses back to Europe, to Copenhagen. I remember Soulshock called me one night and said this new upcoming rapper was interested in cutting the track. We knew who Tupac was, but he wasn't nearly as iconic as he is today. So we were just hyped that we were going to have a real, like, U.S. cut on Interscope. That was even more so the hype for the three of us. We knew that Tupac was clearly an incredible artist. We knew that already.

*Danish producer Soulshock cofounded Soulpower Productions in 1990, and both Ezi Cut and Jay-B released projects on the label.

The story goes that this A & R guy up on Interscope was playing our demo for "Old School," which already had the hook; we had to sample the, like, some vocals from Brand Nubian. The way you hear the song on the record is actually how he was presented for the demo. And allegedly, Tupac walks the hallway and passes the A & R's office, who is in there bumping our song. And he kind of passes the office and then kind of stops and backs his way into the office and goes, "What is *that*?" So his inspiration was telling us the story about how he came up and those who came before him.

Initially, having an Interscope cut made me move to the States. I was there for seven years. But before that we were traveling back and forth. I'd be stationed over there and staying in the Valley for a month and then going back to Europe. We had a clear definition of Tupac. He was definitely an artist that was going to evolve and become somebody. The streets were already buzzing over there. He'd gained some radio play. So everybody's eye was on him, and it was clear to everyone involved this was something special. Not necessarily that he was going to become this iconic rapper decades later, but everybody in the game or trying to get into the game definitely knew who he was. And we especially knew that he was a storyteller.

ERIC ALTENBURGER After I did the Pac album [*Strictly 4 My N.I.G.G.A.Z...*], that's when I sort of became the Rap Guy. To put it in perspective, when I ended up buying my first house, I called it the House That Tupac Built. Everything I got, all the work that came after that, was based on having done that album. It just didn't even matter what it looked like. It's like, "If you're good for Tupac, you're good for us."

With most rappers, you set a call time for ten a.m., you're lucky to get them in by two p.m. They'll come in so deep they need five SUVs. If we have five setups, we'll be lucky to get through two. But with Tupac, I set the shoot for *Me Against the World* at nine a.m., I showed up about a half an hour early, and he was there already. He was by himself just waiting. He understood. It was business. He understood what this meant. *This is for me. I'm promoting myself. I'm working for myself. If I fuck this up, I'm fucking up my own business.* Total professional, super sweetheart. I'm like, *Wow, okay, awesome.*

Then, getting ready for the shoot, doing some setups, I had a stack of CDs. I'm like, "What music should I put on? Public Enemy? Ice-T? Eric B?" He's like, "No, no, no, I brought my own music." Dude puts in the soundtrack to *The Lion King*. All day, on repeat. He just sang it all day. And he was a happy dude. He was being lighthearted. There was lots of smiling. He just had a great personality. Then when it came time for the shoot, boom, street persona. He didn't fake that shit. He lived it. But then he had this sweet, kind side, too.

We did some of that shoot in the studio and went up to the roof to do the rest. When we were up there, he pulled out all these little nickel bags to roll one up with. I was like, "I have some weed over here if you want to try that, instead of who knows what you're smoking there." He was happy about that, and he pulled out $500 and he's like, "Can you get me some of this?" He came by my apartment to pick it up. I had, like, an elevator guy, because it was a prewar building. It was just funny when he came up because he was looking over Tupac's shoulder, looking at me, confused. My wife—who was my girlfriend at the time—was living with me. She's always like, "I just remember him being so clean." He was wearing a Blackhawks jersey. Unmistakable. That was, like, a really classic day for me: hooking up Tupac with my weed guy.

ROB MARRIOTT The feeling of the time was that if you were into hip-hop, if you're part of the culture, you had a very antagonistic relationship with the world. Tupac fully embraced that. He was such a student of the culture that he literally embodied that.

MOE Z MD He wanted to name the album *Fuck the World*. That was his energy. He was thinking about death a lot and it messed us up. A lot of his conversations, talking with me and my sister, he visualized somebody sneaking in on him and shooting him or just getting caught out somewhere. He felt like he had a lot of enemies.

ETHAN BROWN There's a mix of Brooklyn and Queens guys that Pac starts hanging with—Haitian Jack, Freddie Moore, Jimmy Henchman, and Stretch. That relationship kind of starts in the *Above the Rim* era. He's hanging with those guys in '93-ish, and hip-hop is much, much smaller back then. It's tiny. And then the number of guys who would be in hip-hop who had formerly been in the streets in any kind of serious capacity is even smaller. That's how he ends up with those guys.

And in the late eighties and early nineties there's really a decimation of Brooklyn and Queens street guys. Supreme gets indicted and locked up.* The major figures in Brooklyn and Queens—Fat Cat† included—all go down. What's left are folks who are like, *I should get out of this*, and there was a sense that hip-hop was on the up. Mostly because of *The Chronic* in '92.

ALEX ROBERTS I liked Suge and I liked Dre and I loved the music because I knew they were telling the truth. I also knew that the bitches and hoes were bitches and hoes and not somebody's wife or girlfriend. And the end user of this music was mostly Caucasians from the age of thirteen to thirty-five. I knew it would blow up. Dre those first few years—I'd never seen anything like that in my life. I was banging *The Chronic* in demo form, and I grew up in Malibu. Driving in an SL on the PCH, with the top down, cranking it and getting the most dirty looks ever from people that I'd known most of my life.

*Kenneth "Supreme" McGriff was the founder of the Queens gang "the Supreme Team," which at its height in 1987 sold $200,000 worth of drugs per day. McGriff was arrested that year and received a twelve-year sentence. In 2007, he was convicted of ordering the murders of two rivals and imprisoned for life without parole.

†Lorenzo "Fat Cat" Nichols was a Queens drug trafficker who in 1992 pled guilty to ordering the 1985 killing of his parole officer, receiving a maximum state sentence of twenty-five years to life. He also received a forty-year federal sentence for drug distribution and ordering two other killings. He is currently imprisoned at the Clinton Correctional Facility in Dannemora, New York, where Tupac served his 1995 sentence for first-degree sexual abuse.

ETHAN BROWN I talk about *The Chronic* as the *Jaws* of hip-hop. *Jaws* creates basically an entirely new paradigm for movies. Hip-hop is not making a lot of money yet, but the sense is that it could soon be. Guys like Jimmy and Jack are coming into the business, especially because street stuff is in terrible shape.

JUSTIN TINSLEY Think about where Tupac was in the summer of 1993. He's becoming this household name. *Juice* was a cult classic. Pac was already known by the federal government, not just because of his last name, but because former vice president Dan Quayle wanted *2Pacalypse Now* taken off the shelves. *Poetic Justice* is set to hit theaters later that year.

JAKI BROWN Interestingly enough, John Singleton did a movie called *Poetic Justice*. He hired Robi Reed to cast it. I found seventy people for *Boyz n the Hood*, and he didn't hire me to do *Poetic Justice*. At that time, he became a mentee of Spike Lee. Robi Reed had been his casting director for all his films. I think he told John, "You should use Robi because she's my casting director and she's the best." So John never even called me. And they ended up using Tupac, of course.

BARBARA OWENS When I saw *Poetic Justice*, I didn't see anybody or anything else in that film except him.

JUSTIN TINSLEY That role even came with some controversy when you talk about the whole AIDS-test thing.*

SHARONDA DAVILA-IRVING I remember when he first started working on *Poetic Justice*. He was so excited to be

*While promoting the film, Tupac claimed he was asked to take an AIDS test before filming a kissing scene with costar Janet Jackson. In a 2017 interview on the podcast *Drink Champs*, director John Singleton denied the story, claiming, "It was just us talking shit on the set."

working with Janet Jackson. I remember how hurt he was because she was married and her husband came to the set every day. He came to New York and we were celebrating. I was like, "This shit is real. You're really about to be working with Janet Jackson!" He could not wait to get on set with her. Actors always say it's not really romantic. I remember thinking while watching it, *I wonder when he was trying to kick it with her*. I guess he never got the chance.

JUSTIN TINSLEY Now he's in New York filming what will be his third major role, *Above the Rim*, and spending time with these movers and shakers.

CHARISSE JONES On the one hand, you're seeing him in *Above the Rim*, and he's got this amazing career that is taking off, and taking off in a direction that was unprecedented. At that time, you didn't have a lot of rappers who were kind of crossing those boundaries. It was such a surprising thing to see at that time that it was like, *God, I hope he can keep this going. I hope he doesn't shatter that*. I was also starting to worry a little bit that this guy's got the world in his hands, but he's juggling it. What's going to happen?

JUSTIN TINSLEY If you were in New York in the nineties and you were in the know, you knew Haitian Jack. Jack knew all of the party promoters. Jack knew all of the DJs. Jack was fly. Jack was flashy. But also, Ice Cube made it a song, but Jack made it a lifestyle: he was the wrong nigga to fuck with. Jack had no problem putting holes in people. He'd clear out a whole block. Jack's rep was super heavy, but he was charismatic, and Tupac was charismatic. But for all of Tupac's leadership qualities, you could impress him with a lifestyle he wasn't privy to.

ETHAN BROWN Jack was very smooth, very personable, and could ease into different social situations—whether it's the music industry or the downtown New York club scene, which was a big deal. I think he's, like, the most magnetic of all those characters by far. Jimmy [Henchman] is totally different. He is not an amiable person who eases between worlds. He was a super-tough guy—both physically tough and difficult to get to know. So out of that group, I think it's not even close, who you would be drawn to; it's Jack, no question.

If you're Tupac and you're doing *Above the Rim*, these guys are obviously incredible characters to study. I think it's kind of too easy to say he just copies this tough-guy character in *Juice*. It makes much more sense that if your social circle is these guys—whether it's Jack, Jimmy, etc.—that's going to leave a much bigger impression than a fictional character that you're playing. He and Haitian Jack are going around beating up guys together and there's this wild nightclub streak they both have. There are photos of the two of them together with Madonna.

JUSTIN TINSLEY In the 1995 *Vibe* prison interview,* he talked about it: *I was wearing baggy jeans and sneakers and they put me onto designer clothes. I got my first Rolex with them.* And he said that the role of Birdie in *Above the Rim* was inspired by Jack. Hanging around Jack, he picked up the mannerisms Jack had; he was charismatic, but he also instilled fear in a lot of people. He has people in his ear, people like Mike Tyson and Biggie, saying, *Yo,*

*Conducted by journalist Kevin Powell at Rikers Island while Tupac awaited sentencing for his sexual abuse conviction. Powell interviewed Tupac several times during his life.

Pac. Jack is cool, but be careful. You might be out of your league with this one. He's in the major leagues when it comes to street dudes. This ain't some type of dude who is just going to be in awe of you because you're in a movie with Janet Jackson.

It was great, until it wasn't. Pac picked up a lot of game from Jack, and Jack says he really enjoyed hanging out with Tupac. Pac became really embedded in that New York underworld, and once you open Pandora's box, you can't put shit back in there. Eventually, some real street shit is gonna happen, and lines will be drawn in the sand.

The night of the sexual assault incident was November 18, 1993. Literally three weeks before that, Pac is in Atlanta and he shoots two off-duty police officers because he sees them, like, accosting a Black driver. At that point in time, you would think that him shooting two off-duty police officers would be the biggest legal hurdle. But that November, he's introduced to Ayanna Jackson at Nell's [a nightclub in New York].

Allegedly, they go to a corner of the club to perform oral sex. Then they go back to his hotel and they have consensual sex. I think that part is pretty much accepted. Everything after that is all about who you choose to believe.* I truly believe—and I'm not exercising any hyperbole when I say this—this is the single most impactful, consequential case in rap history. Because the chain of events that happens after November 18 alters the course of rap.

ROB MARRIOTT Unlike, say, Mike Tyson, who had a famous rape case around that same time,[†] it was harder to defend Mike Tyson than it was to defend Tupac. Tupac had a track record of being someone who was so pro–Black

*On November 18, 1993, four days after the incident at Nell's, Ayanna Jackson returned to Tupac's hotel suite. The two were there with Tupac's road manager Charles "Man Man" Fuller, Haitian Jack, and a friend of Jack's who remained unidentified. Jackson claimed that she was forced to perform oral sex on Tupac while Jack undressed her and then was forced to perform oral sex on Jack's friend while Tupac held her down. Tupac claimed that he left the room when the other men came in and didn't see what happened after. Jackson sought out hotel security, and Tupac, Haitian Jack, and Fuller were arrested. The unidentified man was never located.

†In February 1992, Tyson was convicted of rape and sentenced to ten years in prison. He was paroled after three years.

women and someone who didn't need to force himself onto women. Having a lot of admirers was part of his persona. It was harder to believe the allegations against him. It was really about trying to respect the woman involved, but there were so many stories behind the scenes that it didn't seem like the truth had come out. There's a lot of weirdness where Haitian Jack was in the room, but he wasn't prosecuted.* There was a lot of whispering about what went down in the hotel room and at Nell's and all of the salacious details of those couple of nights. So it was really trying to suss what was true and what was not, while also defending Pac's right to a fair trial.

RICHARD DEVITT I lived in Manhattan for nearly twenty years, ending in 2002. I lived virtually on the same street, West Fifteenth Street, right near Union Square, for that entire time. If you live in Manhattan, you're called to jury duty quite a lot, because there aren't that many people who actually live in Manhattan. It's like 750,000. There are a lot of courts there—federal, state, and local; civil and criminal—and there are grand juries, so you're constantly being called. So this was one of a number of times that I was called to jury duty.

At that time, I was in my midforties. I was going through my midlife crisis. My musical interests at the time tended much more toward punk rock. I was hanging around with a lot of musicians in the East Village. I was very much into that music scene there. So I wasn't really much of a hip-hop fan. I was sort of neutral on the subject. I didn't know about Tupac. I knew who he was. I knew that the police didn't like him. I knew he was a music star. I wouldn't have recognized his music if you played it.

*On November 24, 1993, Tupac, Haitian Jack, and Fuller were indicted on sexual abuse and sodomy charges. Tupac and Fuller were also indicted on weapons charges for two handguns found at the hotel suite. Haitian Jack's lawyer sucessfully argued that his case should be tried separately, since he wasn't included in the weapons charges. Following the conviction and sentencing of Tupac and Fuller, Haitian Jack's indictment was dismissed and he plead guilty to two misdemeanors. According to writer Connie Bruck, in her 1997 profile of Tupac for *The New Yorker*: "When I asked Melissa Mourges, the assistant district attorney who had tried the case against Tupac, why Haitian Jack had been dealt with in such a favorable way, she said that Ayanna Jackson was 'reluctant to go through the case again.' Jackson had, however, brought a civil suit against Tupac following the trial. (The suit was subsequently settled.)"

A reminder of the way New York State law works: the jurors all had to be from the same county in which the crime occurred. Okay, Manhattan is its own county. It's New York County. And so everyone on the jury was a Manhattanite.

There were two older women on the jury. One of them, this older Jewish lady, was really non compos mentis. She was really not fit to be a juror. She didn't remember things. It was November, as I recall, and the weather was turning bad, and there were snowstorms coming and the trial had lasted a lot longer than originally anticipated. She wanted to get out of New York and get to her condo in Florida. That's all she cared about—"Can we just vote on this now?" She would vote guilty or not guilty depending on the majority. She didn't care if he was acquitted or not, or on what charge. "Can we just get over this?" She would fall asleep in the middle of the discussions. There was a younger Jewish lady who was a nice lady, who I became somewhat friendly with during the trial, who was sitting right next to her, who turned to me at several points and said, "You know, she's senile. She doesn't know what's going on here." She said it loud enough for everybody to hear, and the old lady, who had thick glasses on, she wouldn't even react. She wouldn't even know the comment was meant about her.

The other older lady was much more of a force to be reckoned with. I remember during the jury selection, boy, she really wanted to be on this jury. You could just tell, you know, that she wanted to give all the right answers. I had a number of conversations with her over the course of the long period, because we were sequestered. She positioned herself once we got into the jury room at the head of the table, this lady, and she really tried to preside over things even though she was not the jury foreman.

She had worked in Manhattan. She lived in an upper-middle-class apartment complex on the East Side. She was retired. She had never been married. She was a devout, extreme, right-wing Roman Catholic. She was very religious, very conservative, no experience with relations with the opposite sex. Her social knowledge seemed to have been frozen in 1943.

Here was her position on the whole thing: This poor, poor girl. He was her ideal. He was her star. He was her guiding light that she looked up to and she respected and she fully expected him to marry her, and this is how he betrayed her. That was her entire theory of the case, and she never let go of that theory. She was the one who kept us in there forever. Had it not been for her, we would have acquitted on all counts. She was the reason we deliberated for so long. She would not back down an inch, she wouldn't concede a single point.

A younger woman was trying to tell her people do have sex outside of marriage and they even have casual sex without intending to get married. She didn't buy that. This was too nice of a girl for that kind of thing. She knew there were trashy girls who did trashy things, there always were—that's how she would frame it; this was not that kind of a girl. You could see how well dressed this girl was, and she worked at the Brooklyn Navy Yard, and she was well presented, and she was very soft-spoken, and she's not the kind of girl that would have sex unless she was absolutely determined that she was going to be marrying this guy, and that's what he must have led her to believe. She was starstruck.

So that was her.

There was another guy there who was a pastor. I don't know if he was Black, Hispanic, or Black-Hispanic. He was my roommate during the sequester. But he and I didn't really speak all that much because he was a very soft-spoken gentleman. He was probably in his late thirties. A bit heavyset, but not overly so. Very nice man. He had a congregation somewhere uptown, I don't remember where.

He was very deliberate. I would say very fair-minded. He would ask questions, but they were always pointed questions. What surprised me was he, in the end, whenever we took a vote, he was always voting in Tupac's favor. When we first sort of introduced ourselves to each other and got to know each other, I thought, *This guy, he's religious, he's from a conservative Protestant sect. He is probably going to be really against this kind of out-of-wedlock thing, and he's probably judgmental of hip-hop and thug life and all of that.* He may have been all those things, but he stuck to the facts all the time.

There was a little NYU girl. She was a white girl. She was twenty-one; shy, but very sweet. She thought the whole thing was ridiculous—that Tupac was on trial for this. "The girl knew what she was doing, and Tupac didn't do anything to her, regardless of what happened with the other guys in the room," she said. The girl never claimed at the time that the manager [Fuller] even touched her. She was like, "What are we trying here?" That was her opinion.

There was a Black woman who was in her late twenties. She vociferously stood up for Tupac. She had many arguments with the older woman [who] sat at the head of the table.

CHARISSE JONES You live the moment now and it's hard to believe in a way. Like, everything was one way and then it changed. Post-change you're like, *How was it ever like that?* That was soooo far before Me Too. It was so far before the reckoning for R. Kelly and these other folks, and the reckoning for R. Kelly took a long time. But at the time, for many, it wasn't even in your rearview mirror, that you should maybe look at it and condemn what this guy had been accused of doing.

RICHARD DEVITT I have to remark upon the fact that times have changed so much, with the Me Too movement and everything, that today, the event that night would be seen as egregious. We've come a long way from when I was a kid, with regard to women and charges of rape. This was the nineties—a long ways from when I was a kid, but we weren't where we are today.

I was not personally very impressed with Tupac's attorney. I don't know about the others in the room because they didn't really express an opinion, but I can just tell you that I myself wasn't terribly impressed, and I thought he could have done a better job. He mainly did the down-and-dirty thing that defense attorneys do in a rape case. It turned out that there was an event that happened at Nell's down the street from where I lived, on Fourteenth Street. [Jackson] had oral sex with Tupac, and Tupac's attorney made her go through what happened between them on the dance floor in very graphic detail. He had her go through that step by step.

"He whispered in your ear, 'Would you like to do this?' and what did you say?"

"I said, 'Yes.'"

"Then what happened?"

"He put his hand on my shoulder and I knelt down in front of him," or along those lines.

"And then what happened?"

"He took out his penis." And her voice got kind of quiet.

"And then what happened?"

"I put my mouth on it."

"And then what? Did you like it?"

And she said, "Yes."

If you've ever been in a courtroom, you may know that the court reporter has no reason to speak up. In this case, she did. And I think it was a statement on her part. When he asked her, "Did you like it?" and the girl said, "Yes," the court reporter said, "I'm sorry, Your Honor, I didn't catch that. Would you have the witness repeat it, please?" And she made her repeat that. The fact that the court reporter did that made quite an impression. It made an impression in the jury room later on, and it made an impression on me at the time.

JUSTIN TINSLEY Obviously, our conversations around rape and sexual assault are night-and-day different compared to what they were in 1993 and 1994. If you go back and read the articles from that time, there were a lot of people, men and women, who sided with Tupac. Even back then, to the people who were really astute and aware of Tupac, he felt like so much more than a rapper. He felt like a ghetto Lazarus to a lot of people. The thought of being remembered as a rapist deeply haunted him. In the Ed Gordon interview,* he says, "I can't leave until people actually know that I am not guilty of this."

*Prior to the trial, Tupac gave an extensive interview to journalist Ed Gordon for BET.

Even still, something happened in that hotel room. Something clearly happened. In the [1995 Rikers Island] *Vibe* interview, he said, "Even though I'm innocent of the charge they gave me, I'm not innocent in terms of the way I was acting. . . . I don't know if she's with these niggas, or if she's mad at me for not protecting her. But I know I feel ashamed—because I wanted to be accepted and because I didn't want no harm done to me—I didn't say nothing."

So there is this level of responsibility there. Regardless of what anyone believes did or did not happen that night, Tupac said it himself: he didn't do enough to stop it. At best, he looked the other way. Those aren't my words. Those aren't your words. These are his exact words.

When we think about this case, like, we've got to look at all entry points, all levels of complexities of it, because it's not just, "Did he do this?" Maybe he didn't. But in his own words, he was complicit in what happened. As the guy that made "Brenda's Got a Baby," that made "Keep Ya Head Up"—we never know how we're going to act in situations until we're put into one. And, at least in terms of that situation, Tupac feared for himself and protected himself over protecting Ayanna Jackson.

ROB MARRIOTT Like everything about Tupac, he had this kind of Gemini nature. There's always an angel and a devil on either shoulder.

ETHAN BROWN For sure this incident is a result of hanging out with that group of people. Not blaming anyone and saying it's Jack's fault or this person's fault, but it appears that this incident really is like the fallout from this world that he's in.

JUSTIN TINSLEY Over the course of 1994, Tupac is telling basically anyone who will listen, "I'm innocent. I did not do this." Whether it's on Arsenio Hall, whether it's Ed Gordon, whether it's outside the courtroom the day before he's shot at Quad. November eighteenth leads to Quad; he's calling out all these street dudes in the media, calling out all the hangers-on. He's like, *All these guys were in the room when this incident happened, why am I the only one on trial?* His angst with that is understandable. But, again, you're in that underworld. There are going to be consequences.

ROB MARRIOTT One of the most incredibly articulate star-power moments for him was him coming out of the courtroom and talking to the press very honestly and openly about his case, and why he thinks this happened, what the dynamics were. He showed he really understood how the media works. It's just such a graceful dance around very difficult subjects. He just asked all these very insightful questions to the media as they were surrounding him coming out of the courtroom, and it was probably that interview that caused the shooting that would happen in Quad Studios later. So he was smart, but not *that* smart.

JUSTIN TINSLEY If he's not calling out Jimmy Henchman by name, he's calling out people that Jimmy Henchman associated with. Tupac's name was in the streets because he'd pissed some very powerful and dangerous people off.

ETHAN BROWN Jimmy said there was some kind of arrangement with Pac to record verses for Little Shawn.

JUSTIN TINSLEY He gets a call from Jimmy Henchman saying, "I want you to be on my artist Little Shawn's record." He got paid like $7,500.

ETHAN BROWN He arranged for Pac to be at Quad at a certain time. Pac was late and Jimmy was so angry—like, *How dare this person*. He's getting progressively madder and he's paging Pac: "Where the fuck are you, man?" I think he starts to fear that Pac is gonna run off with his money. I think it was like $7,000 or $7,500. Pac rolls in hours late with Freddie Moore and a bunch of other folks. If you know Jimmy at all, and I'm sure Pac did, you know this is a person you don't cross. Even on minor stuff, like showing up late. I don't mean to, like, make this villainous portrait of him, but he has a very short temper. He's extremely tough. The slightest disrespect or line-crossing could set him off. So you could see how, if you're Pac, this might end badly for you.

JUSTIN TINSLEY When he goes to the elevator that night at Quad, even he says he felt weird about it. But he sees Lil' Cease and them smoking weed on the balcony and that puts him at ease.

TERRENCE "KLEPT" HARDING I'm in the police footage of the lobby that they showed in the news the next day, standing next to Puff.

We were in the studio recording the album because we were in Quad multiple nights going through shit—which, looking back, now knowing more about music, why the fuck y'all gonna waste twelve hours and all the shit in the studio killing our time? We should have had our lyrics ready.

In Quad, there's a doorway that leads to a ledge where you could look down to the streets, so everybody would go out there. I'm in the control room writing. Big in there, chilling out. Cease went out there to smoke or something. So like ten minutes later, we hear Cease yelling, "Yo, Pac, what up?" He runs out like, "Yo, Pac is downstairs." We ain't thinking nothing. We keep writing. I'd be lying if I said the exact amount of minutes that passed, but next thing we know, Cease comes running back into the room, frantic, like, "Yo, niggas got Pac laid down in the lobby."

We all jump up and run to meet him—me, Big, and Nino Brown go to the elevator. When the elevator comes up, a police officer comes up in uniform and starts looking around, so we don't know what the fuck happened. When we got down to the first floor all we saw was blood smeared on the walls, blood clots on the floor. Soon as we looked to the right, to the door, mad police came out. So they got us hemmed up in the lobby for twenty minutes. Cops went upstairs. Ambulance people went upstairs.

So now, after a time lapse, the elevator door opens and it's Pac in a wheelchair. He's just looking around, of course probably confused. I don't even know how he got an elevator upstairs. Pac is bandaged up, being pushed out. He looked around, and in those days we used to wear a lot of jewelry. He looked around to see us just chillin' as they just rolled him out.

ETHAN BROWN When he was photographed being wheeled out of Quad raising the middle finger—I mean, what an incredible moment. And it's like he knows that that's an incredible moment. Having the wits about you, after getting shot, to give the *Post* the middle finger. He was very aware that the *New York Post* and, to a lesser extent, the *Daily News* were incredibly racist publications. There's the amazing Public Enemy song "A Letter to the New York Post"—"190 years of fucked-up news," or whatever the Chuck D quote was. A Black man giving this publication the finger is an incredibly powerful thing to do, and it was also very much a statement: "I'm alive."

TERRENCE "KLEPT" HARDING He was throwing that middle finger up at the media.

ROB MARRIOTT Being a hip-hop journalist at that time was really 70 percent advocacy of the culture—defending it—and the other 30 percent was documenting it. Because the perception of hip-hop was so skewed. The majority of people in the mainstream, they had no real idea what was going on and why things were developing as quickly as they were.

Tupac was like a perfect example of the misunderstood emcee. At *The Source*, we could see that he was incredibly intelligent and articulate and a truth teller and very courageous, and so on, but for everybody else, all they could see were the court cases. Dan Quayle is saying, "There's no place in society for him." So trying to balance the perspective of who this guy is was a priority.

When you see the headlines in the *Daily News* your first instinct is to be like, *This is not the whole story.* But also you're engaging with the rapper. So you also see the underbellies and all of the things that are not quite right—the things that are not developed or not evolved about the culture as well. Being in the *Source* offices was the most exciting thing and the most depressing thing. You saw all the worst of your heroes and celebrated all of the cultural victories. Tupac did that as well. He disappointed a lot of people along the way. He created situations like the one in Oakland where he got into some scuffle and then a child died in the aftermath.*

*In 1992, Tupac was involved in an altercation in which gunshots were fired, killing a six-year-old boy named Qa'id Walker-Teal who was riding his bike at a nearby playground. Tupac was arrested but released. He would later settle a wrongful death suit brought by Walker-Teal's mother.

CHARISSE JONES I remember the day that he got shot, and I came into the newsroom. They asked me to do the story. It was interesting, because I had a colleague, who was another Black woman, and she was saying, "Well, I just don't want you getting pigeonholed into doing just stories about hip-hop." And I didn't see it that way, because first of all, I did have a wide variety of stories. So that was not happening. But on the other hand, I felt that covering someone like Tupac getting shot and talking about hip-hop, that wasn't being pigeonholed to me, that was the moment. That was a real strong strand in the culture. Being the person to chronicle that, I felt, was a great story.

GOBI RAHIMI While I was back working real estate in Orange County, I met an aspiring music video producer by the name of Tracy Robinson. She had a small production company. Within six weeks, I'd moved to LA and moved in with her, and I started helping her with all the music videos that she was producing. I sort of worked up from the PA to production manager to a producer, and we ended up doing a hundred to a hundred and fifty music videos together. Tracy had been doing some work with Pac and introduced me.

I sort of heard the firsthand stories from Tracy about her experience with him and didn't really know much more than that about him. I think the first time that it really sunk in was when we got the call in the middle of the night when he had been shot at Quad Studios.

She just fell apart, she started crying. And then she kind of went into the story of who he was. Tracy was very protective of her relationship with Tupac. Even though I was her boyfriend, she would only give me bits and pieces. After the shooting, I started doing some homework on him. This is '95, so it wasn't exactly like we had Google. It was minimal intel. But from what I did get on him, I realized that he was cut from a different cloth than most of the artists that we'd worked with.

KHALIL KAIN There was a level of fearlessness. To trust, you have to toss away fear. I thought that was beautiful about Pac. He had the ability to trust people because his fear was something that he had just discarded. He had become comfortable with the idea of his demise. It was inevitable. So why have that be an obstacle to [his] forward motion?

I mean, at the studio in the lobby, they told him to get on his knees. He told them, "Fuck you." Anybody who knows anything about Pac knows that that's real and understands that there's power in that. I watched the videotape of Ahmaud Arbery and felt a large sense of pride in the fact that he fought. He was like, *Nah, if it's today, then it's today, but we 'bout to throw these hands.* That's what Pac gave us.

ETHAN BROWN My feeling is that he gets attacked by these guys in the lobby, he fumbles to defend himself, grabs the gun, and gets shot in the hand, and in fumbling with his weapon he shoots himself in the testicle. Jimmy's in the building. Biggie's in the building. Puffy's in the building. I think he's legitimately like, *What the fuck is going on here?*

CATHY SCOTT The Quad Studios shooting didn't happen at all the way they tried to say it happened. It was just a robbery. That's all it was—a robbery. It wasn't attempted murder. If they were out to kill him, they would've killed him. They just took $35,000 worth of jewelry. And then Tupac shot himself in the groin. He went to grab his weapon and fired it accidentally. I went to the Manhattan police department while I was there at Quad and they told me that.

KARL KANI When Tupac got shot in New York at Quad Studios, his first interview that he did when he got out of the hospital was with *Vibe* magazine. I think the third question, it actually says, "Tupac, how did you feel when you got shot?" And this is exactly what he says: "I didn't know I was shot. All I knew was I could feel the heat of the bullet pierced through my Karl Kani drawers." He correlated what he was wearing in that moment. The connection was that strong.

DR. LEON PACHTER He was shot multiple times. And if I recall correctly, one of them was about around his testicle. So the joke there, at that time, was that instead of Tupac they would call him "one pack."

We took him up to the operating room. It was in the middle of the night. I left to start another operation by ten thirty. And then I got emergency calls for the intensive care unit saying that he pulled out all his intravenous lines, and he checked out of the hospital. He checked himself out after only a few hours. The next day, the *New York Post* had a cartoon: it shows a patient on the operating table—Tupac—and I was the doctor looking up at an X-ray. There's a bullet right in the center of the brain. The caption was: "Mr. Shakur, I want to assure you that no vital organ has been injured." And that was because he just, you know, tore [the IV] out and checked himself out.

People don't usually leave within six or seven hours after they've been shot. Even Curtis Sliwa* didn't leave the hospital after he was shot. But otherwise it was business as usual. In the scheme of things, this is basically what we see—we see gunshot wounds through the liver, through the abdomen, through the heart, through the chest, and through the head. His was relatively minor for what we see, although for the individual, it was obviously a major injury.

I think the people around him were concerned that whoever was out there trying to kill him was going to come to the hospital and, you know, finish the job. And it was kind of like that scene in *The Godfather*, where he's in Bellevue Hospital, and they move him out because the other people are coming to kill him. I'm sure that was going through his mind.

*Founder of the Guardian Angels volunteer crime-patrol group and New York City talk radio host. In 1992, he was kidnapped by two men in a taxi and shot twice in the abdomen but escaped by leaping through a window of the moving car. John A. Gotti was charged with ordering the attack, in retaliation for Sliwa's disparaging his father, Mafia don John J. Gotti, on his radio show, but never convicted.

JUSTIN TINSLEY Keep in mind, Biggie is telling Pac, "Watch who you hang with, bro. I'm from Brooklyn. I know these dudes." He knew about those worlds. When he gets shot, Tupac's mind is all over the place already. He implicates Biggie and Puffy in it.

GREG KADING Pac thought that initially in the immediate aftermath of having his head bashed in—*Puffy and Biggie set me up*. But then you realize in time that that wasn't it.

JUSTIN TINSLEY Paranoia defines so much of Tupac's life because paranoia ran in his family. They were battling the government. A lot of that generational trauma passed on to Tupac, and then of course he experienced his own. I wish he wouldn't have checked himself out of the hospital so early, because Biggie wanted to go see Pac and I think he tried to go see him the next day. He looked up to Tupac. He wouldn't have set him up. I think Tupac knew that in his heart. He was looking for someplace to vent his anger.

TERRENCE "KLEPT" HARDING I came in when Big was just starting Junior MAFIA. He had the team name but he didn't have the players. He didn't have the squad. I stepped in with divine timing. I'm new to running with Big, so it had been maybe a month or two when I first met Pac. Big is like, "Pac is at the Parker Meridien, let's go check him."

So we go to the Parker Meridien, and soon as we get in his room, I'm bugging out. I look all over the floor and it's just maaaaaaad composition notebook papers with lyrics on them. I'm like, *The fuck is up with this nigga?* The shit was like snow. Just papers all over the floor. You know how perfectly you have to rip a page out of a composition notebook? This motherfucker had composition notebook pages all over the floor like garbage. I wonder if he did that purposefully because he knew that Big was coming by.

Pac and Big looked up to each other. Big had a lot

of respect for Pac. Big was like, "Don't take your camera. Don't take no pics with him, man." Because he didn't want to look like he was on some fan shit. Like me; I was excited to be there.

I just happen to glance up at the corner of the room and I see a shrine with candles, and when I look close it's a shrine with candles and a picture of Madonna. I'm like, *This motherfucker got a picture of . . .* , and then come to find out he was fucking her. Yo, this is an ill motherfucker.

After that we went and jumped in my car and I drove him and Big across the bridge to buy weed and we blew down weed in my car. Not a lot of rappers can say they rolled around with Pac and Big in their car blowing weed.

PUDGEE THA PHAT BASTARD In the beginning of his career, he definitely gave swag to Biggie—as much as Puffy did. Puffy was responsible for changing and shaping the whole image, but Pac gave him a lot of games. And there are even songs where Biggie starts to rap like Pac. He affects the whole California, almost Southern swag on several songs because he was trying to do what he thought Pac was doing.

When you're close to someone that's from a different area—at the time, you know, LA, New York—and then they draw a line in the sand, at some point, you get confused, if not shocked, if not angry as fuck, if not vengeful. You start to feel like you woke up one day and you don't know the motherfucker that you've been telling all your secret plans. It kind of becomes an Achilles' heel. I think Pac's biggest issue was not getting the respect, or even just the recognition, when he did all he did to support Biggie, especially in LA. Without quoting the dead, I would just say he was definitely feeling slighted. He felt almost like he had been taken advantage of, used as a stepping stool.

On "Temptations," he says, "Give him the finger," which is the name of my album. So people didn't understand that he was shouting me out everywhere until Angie Martinez asked me about the Biggie beef—when he says my name in the "Hit 'Em Up" video. And I had songs with Biggie. I can joke about it now, but I was driving around looking behind me pulling off the roads. I thought people were following me. It was at a time where people were shooting everybody. So even though I felt so good that my friend said my name, I was like, "You couldn't have said it in 'Dear Mama'?"

ETHAN BROWN In terms of the actual shooting, Jimmy Henchman claims basically total ignorance. But then, you know, this is what was so interesting talking to him. The phrase that he used, you know, I'll never forget it. It was like: "Pac, you were disciplined." I was just like, *What?* Your entire life has been clouded by the allegation that you had Tupac shot, and you're saying, with a tape recorder in front of you, that Tupac got disciplined.

CATHY SCOTT Tupac would not cooperate on the shooting investigation. So they closed the case after a week. I said to them: "Well, when someone dies in a homicide, they can't cooperate with you because they're dead. Do you close those cases because the victim won't cooperate?" It's a hell of a reason, and it's not a valid reason. There's no logic to it. When it came to Tupac, Manhattan police couldn't have cared less.

RICHARD DEVITT Even the older woman who really wanted to crucify Tupac, regardless of whatever he may or may not have done, she even dismissed the gun charges immediately. When we first went into the jury room, the gun charges were dismissed in minutes. The gun that they entered as evidence was a different-colored gun. [Jackson] testified about the gun—she described a gun that was completely different than the gun that they entered into evidence. The gun they entered into evidence was silver colored; she described a black-colored gun. That and various other details about the gun, which I no longer recall, made us immediately discount those gun charges. We all felt, even the most conservative, that the guns had been planted there by the cops. Everybody believed that.

The cops who testified, frankly, I didn't believe a word of what they said. And I don't think any of the jury did either. They just didn't come across as believable and it was felt that they had an ax to grind. I do recall that they admitted to the fact that they were basically stalking Tupac. There were a number of them around the hotel. They were out to get Tupac, and it was obvious. He was in town to make a music video, and they hounded him all over town. Because eventually when he was shot in the middle of the whole thing, they were at his side thirty seconds after he was shot. It was just phenomenal. The feeling was at the time that he was shot by one of the cops. That wasn't discussed in the jury room, but I remember people speculating afterward. We didn't feel that the cops were being fair to him at all.

JUSTIN TINSLEY Of course Tupac is gonna be the one to catch the brunt of everything. He's Tupac Shakur. He'd just shot at two off-duty police officers. The federal government knows who he is and hates him. At some point they're gonna be waiting on you to slip up.

KHALIL KAIN He was being dragged in too many ugly directions by the system. They immediately spotted how he was influencing our culture and made a point of keeping him occupied with lawyer fees, in court, and behind bars. He did not rape that girl. Fuck outta here. That's not in his character. And to talk to him about it was just sickening, to understand the level of persecution.

RICHARD DEVITT We were sequestered in a hotel, a really kind of shabby place. The city of New York didn't have a lot of money. It was a sort of a roach-infested place, like a Holiday Inn, outside Kennedy airport. We were bused there in a police van with our armed guards the entire time back and forth. We actually ate at the place with the guards standing around the table. We all had to be at one big table. They made sure that, like, when we walked in, there were guards standing in front of the newsstand. We didn't look at any newspaper. The TVs were taken out of our room. So we were incommunicado. We had no idea whatsoever what happened. So the next day after it happened, and they came into the courtroom, as always, when we would come into the courtroom, the jury was the last to arrive. We came in and right away we noticed that Tupac was not there.

So the judge turns to us and he says, "Ladies and gentlemen of the jury"—and I'm paraphrasing—"I would like to instruct you that the defendant will be arriving shortly and you are to make no inferences whatsoever about his appearance. You are not to discuss his appearance afterward when you deliberate. His appearance today has nothing to do with the events that occurred during what he's accused of." Then, they wheeled Tupac in in a wheelchair. I was like, *Whoa, what happened here?* So we kind of glanced at one another. I remember being incredibly curious as to what went on. But it didn't have any effect on our deliberations. Nobody speculated on it in the jury room. Nobody called attention to it.

WENDY DAY As the founder of Rap Coalition, I kind of took it upon myself, wherever there was a need in rap that I could fill, I kind of stepped up and filled it. That kind of became my self-imposed job description. I knew Pac was in trouble. I knew he was going to court. I knew that something had transpired at Quad Studios, and I knew he was scared, because he ran. I kind of knew about the issues. I didn't know any of the inner workings of those issues. I just knew he was in trouble and he needed help. His concerns were legitimate. It wasn't just his perception. It wasn't as bad as he thought, but it also was very real.

Of course, I didn't know that at the time; I just assumed that it was real. I didn't really know any details. And I had had a relationship with the Nation of Islam since the very early days of Rap Coalition. The Fruit of Islam* always stood out because they were always super respectful. They wore suits and red bow ties. They were very security minded. We hired them for a lot of events, so I had a relationship with a gentleman named Brother Arthur, and when Tupac first had the situation occur at Quad Studios, I called Arthur and asked if there was anything he could do to help him, and he did.

*The Nation of Islam's security force.

RICHARD DEVITT Another of the jury members was a skinny white guy. In the jury room, he would go into the bathroom repeatedly. Finally, the younger Jewish lady who was sitting next to me, she said, a couple of days into it: "Have you ever noticed how he does that?"

It was toward the end of things now, and after not really playing much of a role, he suddenly wanted things to get going. "Let's just wrap this up. Let's wrap this up. Let's take another vote. Let's take another vote." She said, "Well, you know why he's doing that?" She said, "He's a crackhead." We weren't sequestered from the beginning. We were sequestered partway along. But she said, "He's running out of drugs. That's the reason why he's in a hurry to end this."

We—with the exception of the Catholic lady and her old-lady friend who would sometimes join her—repeatedly voted to acquit on all the charges because it was felt that Tupac wasn't even in the room when the abuse occurred. Whether somebody else or the rest of them gang-raped or not is irrelevant to this case.

So we thought Tupac was definitely not guilty of anything at all. We were very close to saying hung jury. Hour after hour after hour; you have no idea how tedious it was. We actually sent a note out at one point that said, *We're having difficulty coming to a decision, Your Honor.* We wanted to know about how a hung jury would work. He sent a note back that said keep going. After that, we went a whole other day with this woman.

I said, "This is ridiculous. This is not going anywhere. We cannot make a decision here. Let's just say a hung jury."

A lot of people threw up their hands and said, "All right."

The old lady said, "Wait, wait, wait, wait, wait, does this mean he's going to go free?! Is that what you people want? He's got 'Thug Life' written on his stomach. Is that what you want? Somebody like that roaming the streets?"

She gave this nearly hysterical speech about how there'll be other women who are victimized and the message we were sending to young people. She was virtually arguing that whether this guy is guilty or not guilty, the details of this case are virtually irrelevant. Because it's the message that you're going to be sending that's the key. She said, "I will not allow you to say this is a hung jury."

We were like, "Listen, we're just not going to go any further, okay?"

She said, "There's the fourth-degree thing, you have to admit that something did happen to this girl, right?"

Our knowledge of fourth-degree sexual assault was that if you put your hands on somebody in a bar or something like that, that's fourth-degree sexual assault. People went around the table and said things like, "Well, how much time will he get for a conviction like that?" I think we may have even sent a note out to the judge asking about that. The answer came back that he can't talk to you about the sentencing or the sentencing potential. That's irrelevant. You're to judge the facts of the case and the facts only.

The feeling among the majority of people was that, *Well, this is a pretty minor charge. Did he really get four years for that?**

As the judge was wrapping up, he turned to the jury,

*On December 1, 1994, Tupac and Fuller were convicted of first-degree sexual abuse, a Class D felony defined as, per the *Washington Post*'s reporting on the conviction, "nonconsensual groping or touching." The sentencing options ranged from probation to seven years imprisonment. On February 7, 1995, Justice Daniel P. Fitzgerald—remarking, "This was an act of brutal violence against a helpless woman"—sentenced Tupac to one and a half to four and a half years in prison. Fuller, who had no previous criminal record, received four months in prison and five years' probation.

and he said, "There's no law preventing you from speaking to the press, but I would like to tell you that it's not a very pleasant experience. You may find that there's personal repercussions from having that kind of visibility. So, if you wish, I would advise you to leave the courtroom by one of the side doors so you don't encounter the press who are waiting outside. You've been sequestered, so you don't realize that there will be TV cameras and print reporters and a lot of press there."

Most of the jury went out one side door and avoided the press. This NYU girl and I, I don't know why, but we chose the other side. When we came out the door, boom, there we were, just me and her in front of this whole scrum of reporters and cameras and lights.

She was scared and she put her arm around my waist. One of the reporters said, "Is this a sequestered-jury love story like we had in the Bernie Goetz trial?"*

I said, "No, no, no, no, no. We're just friends."

So I did most of the talking, and she just kept her arm around my waist and she was shivering, she was so scared, but it was cold, too.

The reporter for MTV was right in the middle of the scrum in the front. He went down on one knee and held out his microphone to me. I was sort of aiming my comments at him because he was the one right in front of my face. First thing he asked me was: "There were two older women on this jury. Do you feel that the two older people were really competent to understand the music and the culture behind hip-hop?"

I, perhaps suffering from Stockholm syndrome myself, was far too generous to these two old ladies. I did not want to throw a wrench into the works and get myself

*After the 1987 trial of Bernard Goetz for shooting and injuring four Black teenagers on a New York City subway car, two jurors—twenty-seven-year-old James Mosley and thirty-three-year-old Diana Serpe—became romantically involved. "All I can say is go to jury duty, you never know what might happen," Mosley told the Associated Press following the verdict, which acquitted Goetz of attempted murder charges.

in trouble by saying one of them was completely senile and had no idea what was going on most of the time— seriously, she did not—and the other one wanted to lock up every Black male that she could get her hands on. I was far too generous. I said, "Well, you know, there were two older women here, but remember, this is Manhattan. They're not completely unsophisticated. They know a little bit more about the world." That was wrong. I don't know why I said that. Maybe because I was trying to protect them or protect the jury.

In retrospect, would I have said anything different? Probably not, because of the implications. It might have ended up in a mistrial had I said, "Listen, one of them was senile, another one was probably a crackhead, the other one wanted to crucify Tupac no matter what." I just didn't think that was the appropriate thing to say, even though it was the truth.

I said that, and unbeknownst to me, I was on every local news broadcast that night and I was on *MTV News* with Kurt Loder. My brother lives in Pennsylvania. He was shaving the next morning and he said he had on MTV and all of a sudden he said, "I heard your voice from the other room."

CHARISSE JONES I think that it was a very racialized paradigm. I think that because he was hated by cops, because he was this fledgling rap icon becoming a movie star, there was a protectiveness around him, which obviously does a great disservice to the woman who was abused. I think there's been a real awakening since then with R. Kelly and all of that, but at that time, I feel that Black women felt that they had to be loyal to this young brother. Even though they were, in doing that, denying the humanity and the emotion that this young woman had to be going through, having experienced this terrible assault. I got the sense that people were kind of Team Tupac, especially because he was a young Black man who was being vilified by some in the white community.

RICHARD DEVITT As soon as I got back to work, I hadn't even gotten my coat off when three Black women walked into my office and shut the door behind them. They were furious at the girl. My own secretary, Michelle, was from Queens. She said, "What the hell is wrong with that girl? She walks into a room, there's five men there and there was a gun on the table. Why the hell didn't she just turn around and walk out of there?" They were vehemently in support of Tupac and they were mad at me for convicting him. I said, "Listen, I wanted to acquit on all charges. Most of the people in the room did. There were a couple of people there that kept us there forever. And so that's what we ended up with." Still, the MTV reporter had asked if the verdict was a compromise, and he was right. It was a compromise.

PUDGEE THA PHAT BASTARD After the shooting, he changed. He was more guarded. Not with me, but I could feel him being darker.

MOE Z MD I was supposed to be at that session when he got shot at Quad. I was in the studio doing something else. And I couldn't even break away. It was rough living with each other after that.

D-SHOT I think he never got over when he got shot up in New York. I think he felt like he was betrayed and let down out there. He'll pull up on you. He'd get on the plane and go there and get there expecting you to be a real dude and take care of him. Apparently somehow he got caught up out there and he can never live that down. So he started lashing out in his music; you can hear it in his music. The anger and all the stuff behind that.

MOE Z MD He was really depressed about how he was for the women and lifting them up. And then this girl was saying that he raped her. And he didn't. He told me that whole story, too. He was just really frustrated with how all that was going down—people being against him.

PUDGEE THA PHAT BASTARD The rape case is the beginning of him understanding how poisonous this world is. He didn't become vapid but he definitely became short with people more, and was way more selective. There weren't as many people hanging around. But our relationship was one of authenticity. I just was gonna be brutally honest. He appreciated your honesty. There's no component to stop me from saying something is some bullshit, and he was the same way.

ALEX ROBERTS When I told my lawyer I'd met Pac, he said, "Don't ride any elevators with him." When I saw Pac the next time after Quad, I brought it up.

"Is there going to be retaliation?"

He goes, "If I ever run into them."

I go, "What if you don't need to run into them?"

He said, "Why would you want to be involved?"

"I'm not involved," I said. "You know who your mom runs with, right? Well, have you ever seen the name Calabrese on some of the garbage trucks?"

"I have."

I go, "That's my mother's maiden name."

"Oh shit! You're the real deal. You're a real OG."

I said, "Fuck you, man. I'm not that much older than you."

He liked that. We both spoke our mind with a bit of an attitude.

KHALIL KAIN I mean, the shit he said to the judge—that he's not trying to get less time and he's not trying to be part of the system; the system is fucked*—you can't go into court and tell them that. But he did that anyway.

MOE Z MD He was thinking about signing us to his label Out Da Gutta† and merging our label with his. I said, "Man, we can even demo stuff in my studio and the crib so you don't have to spend money and reinvent it in the studio." He never got to do that because of the situation with him going to jail.

KHALIL KAIN My cousin was there while he was there. My cousin asked me about him: "What's good? Do we look out for him?" I'm like, "Make sure nothing happens to that muthafucker, man."

ETHAN BROWN The thing that always struck me about that case is that he gets sent up to Dannemora. That's a

*During the sentencing hearing, Tupac told Justice Daniel P. Fitzgerald: "I mean this with no disrespect, Judge—you never paid attention to me. You never looked into my eyes. You never used the wisdom of Solomon. I always felt you had something against me." In her turn to address the court, Jackson—according to reporter George James's account of the sentencing for the *New York Times*—described how "she has received threatening phone calls, lives in constant fear, has suffered nightmares and, while Mr. Shakur 'has been glorified by his peers and fans,' she has been viewed as a villain. Calling for a stiff sentence, she concluded, 'He should not be allowed to use his so-called celebrity status to avoid the consequences of his actions.'"

†Tupac's Interscope imprint.

terrible state prison. My feeling is that being sent upstate destroyed his life. I think he's deeply traumatized by that prison, and I think it puts him directly into the arms of Suge. He's angry. He's traumatized. His career has really taken this mega blow. That sequence of events seems like the most important part of the story.

STELLA NAIR *So Pumacahua, who is originally from Chinchero, is the one who leads the capture of Túpac Amaru II. In the end, he regrets it, and he goes against the Spanish and he also dies. You would think that the people of Chinchero in particular would maybe have some ambiguity. On the church, there's a picture showing a lion and a dragon fighting—Pumacahua, a name referencing the puma, and then Tupac is the serpent. So that battle is memorialized. But they all side with Túpac Amaru II and his legacy. And it really symbolizes indigenous persistence.*

VII

WENDY DAY After I connected Pac with the FOI [Fruit of Islam], I forgot about it. My intention wasn't for anybody to know that I had asked [the FOI] to help him. It wasn't anything more than just offering help because I had access and I saw somebody in need. But I guess somebody told Pac, because later I got a letter from Rikers, from him, thanking me for securing him. "It's nice to know that somebody respects my music so much that they would do this for me." And, you know, when I read that, I thought about that time I was standing in line at the Palladium. I was not necessarily a fan of his music. I did it for him because I would have done it for any rapper. For some reason, I felt obligated to tell him that, and I don't know why. Age brings wisdom. If it had transpired today, I would have just let it go. But back then my attitude was, *How dare he misconstrue my actions?*

In a response letter, I basically said to him, a lot of what you do you bring upon yourself, and then you complain in the media that people are profiling you, because, you know, you're a rapper, but, you know, my experience of you is you were so loud and obnoxious in line to get into a club that I had to get off the fucking line and move to the back, putting myself in a worse position to get in. At that point in time, I think I was only really aware of a couple of his songs. And I explained to him that I [helped him] because I saw he was in need, and I would have done it for anybody. So, a couple weeks later, when a letter came back to me with his return address, my initial response in my head was like, *Oh, he's gonna crush me.* But when I read the letter, it was so respectful. I think it started "Dear Queen," and it was so humbling. He came so opposite of what I thought. He was peaceful and he thanked me again for what I did. And the amazing part to me was that he understood what I was saying. I mean, he really understood.

His response was: *Here's where I come from. This is the kind of life I had. Here's why I'm the way I am.* It was very genuine, and he really put himself out there. I wrote back to him, and I came as humble and as open as he did. We just started to discuss things back and forth. I sent him a box of books; I was only able to send one or two boxes, I can't remember which, because he got caught smoking weed pretty soon thereafter, and they killed all his packages, but I sent him some of my favorites and then we corresponded about those books. I sent him *The Prince* by Machiavelli, Richard Wright's *Black Boy*, *Afrocentricity* by Dr. Molefi Asante. At first he was a little bit shocked because I'm white and I had sent him some very Afrocentric books, but that's what I like and that's where the lyrics at the time were taking me. That was my education at that point in time. I think he was kind of amazed by that. Because he had been so vulnerable with me and I had shown my vulnerability to him, it really developed a friendship.

ANGELA ARDIS I worked in the marketing department at Junior Achievement* in 1995. I was doing a little bit of acting, a little bit of modeling. Nothing heavy. We were putting together the board books and MC Lyte's "Ruffneck" came on—it was about ten thirty at night; we had had a long day. We got up and we danced or what have you and they were like, "If you could have a roughneck, who would you want?" I said Tupac. My roommate at the time said Treach, and so then somehow it became a situation where they bet that I couldn't get in touch with Tupac. And I said of course I can't. He's in jail—a celebrity in jail at that. I left it alone. I didn't think any more about it.

*A nonprofit youth organization that delivers learning programs.

Went to bed that night and woke up the next morning and my roommate is like, "So how are you going to get in touch with Tupac? You have to do this bet." My whole day, I was hearing Tupac. Everywhere I went, I was hearing Tupac. I said, *Okay, I'm into signs and "the universe" and all these things.* I had an uncle who's in jail, and I knew you needed the prison number [to write to an inmate]. He's at Rikers Island. If I call Rikers Island, will they give me his prison number? I had to call information. They gave me the Rikers Island phone number. A nice lady answered the phone. And five seconds later, I had Tupac's prison number and the Rikers Island address. I'm a Gemini, too. So my mind is spinning. How is he going to find my letters? I'm thinking he's getting bags and bags of mail—that if it was that easy for me, there's thousands of people who know how to do that already.

I said, *I'm going to get a colored envelope.* I went to Kinkos the next morning and when I looked at all the colors that they had on display, the fuchsia one stuck out.

I bought the one envelope, very happy with my purchase. I came home and wrote out a letter. I typed it when I got to work. I put a picture of myself in there. I put my phone number in there, and I FedExed it off using the company FedEx and didn't think about it again. I sprayed a little perfume on the envelope, like, *That'll be cute.*

Two or three days later, I went on a date and there was a message on my machine when I got home. "Hey, this is Tupac." I ran across the house to my roommate's room and completely destroyed her life. I'm like, "You got to wake up. Tupac is on my machine." I had a machine that rewinds itself back to zero, but I didn't think it was actually gone because nothing has been recorded over it yet—it was one of those little cassettes. I said, "We've got to go to the job and get the recorders that we have there." She was like, "Are you kidding me?" We went and we couldn't find the recorder. So I didn't have that. That would have been the most amazing thing, to still have that recorded. But I wasn't thinking about anything. I was just super excited that he even got the letter.

WENDY DAY We talked about me running Rap Coalition as a white person and how difficult that was, and, you know, what his plans were in life and what he wanted to do. Because of my savvy on the business side, we talked about how his business manager—I think Mutulu Shakur was the person handling his finances—how terribly he was doing financially, how much he owed in taxes, how much he owed to so many people. And this was not foreign to me, because in the industry that's very accurate. When you're struggling to come up, you actually owe more than you have and it's just sort of the nature of the music business. It's kind of like getting out of college and you go to get your first job and you've got all this friggin' debt from your student loans. The music industry is kind of the same way: you've got all this debt that you have to pay off before you can really start to succeed. That was a source of frustration for him, because he had songs that so many people knew, yet behind the scenes, he was struggling, and he just couldn't come to grips with that; he couldn't really understand how that was possible.

ANGELA ARDIS I really did think he was a roughneck. That's how they painted him. But I remembered watching an interview that he did and it was just something in his eye. There was something else in there. I knew it was thug this and thug that, but there's a real person in there. There's somebody's baby boy in there. I used to say, "I think he needs a hug." If you look at his interviews before he became Tupac, when he was talking about the school that he used to go to, it's a completely different guy.

MARK ANTHONY NEAL I think Tupac contemporaries understood what he was trying to do with "THUGLIFE."* I think it was important to Tupac at the time, because he knew that it was language that would resonate with people that he was trying to connect with.

 I don't think we've ever had a problem being called thugs. But the white framing of what a thug was didn't represent the fullness of how we thought about it in the context of our communities. So what he attempted to do was to take this word that we knew already had so many

*An acronym that stood for "The Hate U Give Little Infants Fuck Everybody."

multiple meanings and framings within Black communities, and tried to actually theorize about what that meant.

None of that was ever going to move white folks from seeing a bunch of young Black kids and calling them thugs, or more importantly, older Black folks seeing a group of younger Black folks [and] calling them thugs. What you get there is an example of the way that Tupac was a conceptual thinker. How he talks about thugs was the first draft of him working through conceptually how to balance who Black folks are as humans, who Black men are as humans, along with all these other kinds of pressures that we all know Black men are dealing with on a daily basis.

ANGELA ARDIS As we started exchanging letters I was struck by his vulnerability—the swiftness with which he was open. And maybe that's how he normally was; I didn't know. First of all, I wasn't expecting any letters, and then when they started coming, especially when he wasn't getting mine—when they moved him, he thought I'd given up on him. I always call it a connection. He didn't love me. I didn't love him. There was love for each other per se. It was not a love thing. It read like it could have been something magical, but I think that it was more of him needing something while he was in there. The level of his poetry and all that kind of stuff was surprising. I wasn't expecting any of that. He is the only person in my entire life that I've ever had what I would consider a platonic situation where it was completely mental.

In the process, I learned he wasn't who I thought he was, but then it became kind of sad, knowing that you're trapped inside of something that you wish you could change. I think that, had he had the ability to stay and clean some house, he would have found another level, and how people see him now would have shifted.

WENDY DAY Pac had just hired Charles Ogletree, a professor from Harvard, and he felt like this guy could really get him out of jail. He was sharing that with me, and he was really excited about it. But it made me a little sad because he had been incarcerated at that point like eight or nine months. I kept thinking to myself: *You just not only wasted nine months of your life but nine months of your life at a time where your album had just dropped.* And back then, history taught us that if you weren't out and about to work your record, it would tank. His record didn't tank; it actually did quite well. But it could have done so much better if Pac had been out and about to be able to market and promote himself. And that kind of pissed me off.

It was like, "Well, if all of a sudden they're saying that, okay, you're not really guilty, and they're going to let you out, who's going to compensate you for that fuckery that you just went through deemed incarceration?" And his response was, "I'm just gonna ask the judge for credit." I found that so funny, because it showed me that, first of all, he knew that at some point, something was going to happen where he would get in trouble again. Not because he was a troublemaker; because he was so honest and outspoken, and because of that he would absolutely get into trouble.

ANGELA ARDIS I think that Tupac was trapped between two worlds. It would be complicated. It was a time when you had to be as real as what you were rapping about. I think eventually he got caught up in that game. Then the people around you are telling you what you need to do and be. On the flip side, you have who you probably really are, and you really just want to take care of your people. And you're torn. I think jail for him was a time to sit and reflect and figure out what he was trying to do. But society put this hat on him, and he felt he had to wear it when he was being seen by them.

WENDY DAY He was actually very upbeat. He was very aware of his star status. And he was very aware that people treated him differently because of that—in a good way and in a bad way. Other guys would give him extra food or access to their commissary. So he saw the good side of it. But he also saw the bad side of it. When I went to visit him, they sat us at the very first table right near the guard tower. They didn't do that because he was a bad prisoner; they wanted to sit there and eavesdrop for their own entertainment. And he told me that, as we were sitting right there. He's like, "I wonder if I should be speaking a little bit louder, so that homeboy can actually hear me." It was very aware and very funny, but he knew what it was. It surprised me how much of a fame seeker he was. Not to say that was problematic, but he loved the idea of dating Janet Jackson. He loved the idea of Mickey Rourke coming to visit him. When they told him, "Okay, there's an older white woman here to see you," he thought it was Madonna.

It took him a minute to come out. I probably sat there for like twenty minutes, waiting for him to come out to the visit. He went and took a shower. When he came out, he was kind of laughing. He's like, "Man, if I'd known that was you, I wouldn't have taken a shower. I thought it was Madonna coming to see me." I'm like, "Hey, I'm worth a shower!" The fact that he could say to a guard, "Hey, let me go just shower real quick, before you bring me out," tells me what kind of power he had inside of a maximum-security prison.

KENDRICK WELLS While he was free, everybody's like, "We got your back. We got your back." But once he went to prison, it was people like Madonna who offered him things, who got things for him. He learned that it wasn't about race. It was about people who really cared. Some people were very genuine; Madonna was very genuine. He wanted me to know that. He wanted me to know love comes in from places you don't expect.

ANGELA ARDIS Meeting Tupac in prison was surreal. It was a little challenging for me only because there were other people there. Thug Life showed up and I didn't know any of those guys. They're sitting there with me. And then he walks in. I left to go to the vending machine. I hear the gate, and the doors opening and closing and footsteps, and I think I'm about to pass out. He came in. He was a lot smaller than I thought he would be. The bald head wasn't there, of course—he's in jail. The picture you have in your head—he's not coming with the leather vest on and the bald head with the bandanna around it and the earrings. But the calmness of him, his demeanor, his tone, was the same as the letters. The conversations that we had weren't as exciting as the letters; that's a little difficult to reenact per se. But then again, the other guys were there and they were having conversations with him, too, so it was kind of like trying to appease two things at one time. You have the situation where we're soft and cuddly over here and then it's back over there talking about business.

PUDGEE THA PHAT BASTARD My letters to Pac in jail were— I don't want to say generic, but they were very "keep your head up." In fact, in one of them, I used all his songs to write the letter. His songs became my tools to communicate. I knew the things that other people were writing—"Yo, that shit is fucked up." "How these bitches going to do that to you?" "How you gonna get locked up for rape?" "How are they gonna shoot—?" "What the fuck is the label doing about this?" I'm gonna stay on the fringes until you need something from me. He wrote me back three times, and all of our letters were generic. Our calls were more so on the fun side, because we would talk about people and say things that we wouldn't normally say—things that I cannot repeat here.

MOE Z MD I sat in on the session he did with Richie Rich and Mike Mosley.* There's a song where Jasmine Guy[†] is singing on the hook. This was after Pac was already in jail, and my sister and I were vocal-coaching her for the record. I remember going to Johnny J's[‡] house and working on something that was supposed to be Outlawz and Thug Life together.

We tried to get him on one of the songs where it was all of the Outlawz and all of Thug Life. He was going to do his part from jail. We had the phone on speaker in the studio in the vocal booth with a mic on it. We had

*Bay Area rapper and producer, respectively.

[†]Entertainer and star of the TV series *A Different World*, on which Tupac guest-starred in 1993.

[‡]Multiplatinum songwriter and Death Row producer who died in 2008.

the other phone to the speaker, so that he could hear the beat. But the music sends that delay to him. And then there's a delay coming back to us at the same time, and we hear in all of it. So I was like, "Dang, Pac, I don't think we're gonna be able to make this work." He hung up. That was the last time I talked to him.

ANGELA ARDIS The thing that I love about the letters, based off of the responses that I have gotten over the years, is that it allows people an opportunity to see him through his own words. I didn't tell you anything about Tupac myself. He was telling you; you were learning as I was learning. You got an opportunity to see something else.

KENDRICK WELLS I went to jail in '92 and then I didn't talk to him again until like '94. I had heard he went to jail. Somebody gave me his number and his address. I wrote to him; he was still happy to hear from me. We talked about how we fell off. He told me where he was coming from. I told him where I was coming from. We were excited. It was like he needed a sense of foundation—a sense of reality. By the time I got to him at Death Row, he was already, like, completely floating above reality.

JUSTIN TINSLEY Suge goes to Tupac in jail, basically saying, "We have a common enemy." I don't even know how deep Pac's hatred was. I know he was upset. But Tupac could be manipulated. Like, as iconic as he is, he was still twenty-four years old sitting in a maximum-security penitentiary—in his eyes, for a crime he wasn't guilty of.

So there's gonna be rage boiling up in there, and then you have the stories about the guards maybe assaulting Tupac, so he's dealing with that. The dude is a ticking time bomb. He just needed someone to pull the pin out of the grenade and throw him in somebody's direction. Suge was that dude.

STELLA NAIR *The Spanish recognized at the moment of Túpac Amaru II's uprising how powerful cultural and artistic production is from indigenous people, and that these things are active symbols and a threat to Spanish rule. At the end of this horrific eight-hour public execution, they say you can no longer dress in Inca clothing, you can no longer have portraits of your Inca ancestors, you can no longer speak Quechua. Everything that gives them indigenous identity and shows their continuity to the greatness of the past is illegal.*

The Inca believe when you die you just transition physically, but you're still alive, so your mummy has to survive. Once the Spanish realize the power of these mummies, they go out and try to destroy them. Around that time, indigenous portraits really take off, particularly of rulers, and these are seen as the new way in which those ancestors live and exist. So for indigenous people, those would have been very potent symbols, but from a European perspective, they were just portraits.

Materiality is really important: it doesn't matter the form something is in; the materials carry the essence of something. There's this whole different way of understanding the power of the visual, material world that was very different from a European perspective.

"Huaca" is the Quechua word for anything sacred. Throughout the colonial period, in the extirpation of idolatry, as the Spanish called it, you see them struggling to figure out what items are huacas. It's a totally different way of understanding the world around you.

And all those things come to a head around Túpac Amaru II's execution, where suddenly they're like: It is all these things. And all these things are a threat to our ability to control the Andes.

VIII

VIRGIL ROBERTS Before I started work at SOLAR,* one of the passions I had was doing civil rights litigation. I represented the NAACP in a Los Angeles school desegregation case. That was my own personal passion for which I didn't get paid any money. So I did things to make money. One of the things that I started doing was work representing people in the music industry. In the late seventies, there probably were no more than maybe fifteen Black lawyers in the country that did music work. I started to represent a lot of the Black clients in Los Angeles. There were groups like the Sylvers, and Cheryl Lynn, and the Whispers—all of whom I represented. Most of the artists on the SOLAR label were my clients. As a consequence, I got to know Dick Griffey, who was the owner and the founder of SOLAR Records, really well. He was a very Afrocentric man, and so was I.

So as this company became really successful and was getting ready to expand, Dick came to me and said, "Hey, want to be our in-house lawyer?" Initially, I was like, "No." In 1979, the voters in California passed a proposition that had the impact of doing away with desegregation litigation in California. When the voters passed Prop 1, those of us in the civil rights community, we tried

*Los Angeles–based R & B and soul record label founded in 1977 whose artists included the Whispers, Calloway, and Babyface.

173

to get that proposition overturned, on the grounds that it was a denial of equal protection. We lost. Then I decided that if I wanted to become involved in doing public school reform, I had to do it in another way. And that meant becoming more involved with nonprofit organizations and other things. The life of a litigator doesn't allow you to become involved in the community, because the court controls your time. So I talked to my clients like the Whispers and Leon Sylvers. They all thought it was an okay thing for me to work for the record company. They loved the idea that their lawyer would now be at the record company. So I left private practice and started working for SOLAR late 1981, early 1982.

Philosophically, it was a good place to be. I mean, Dick, he wanted to have Black people or people of color do everything for him. And that was consistent with my own personal philosophy. And so I went to work there and stayed for like fourteen years. Dick was a real entrepreneur. So the work that I did was negotiating and drafting contracts, and was also overseeing various business operations. When I started, I was vice president of SOLAR Records and president of Dick Griffey Productions. And Dick Griffey Productions was the largest Black concert promoter in the country. We did literally all the big Black tours. We took Michael Jackson out on tour. We had a whole concert promotion company, we had a personal management company, we had two publishing companies. And all those companies are kind of under the Dick Griffey Productions rubric itself. I was both a lawyer in the sense of doing deals, but also the CEO in terms of managing people in the companies and our relationships with banks.

Dick believed that Black folks should own what they

create. There's actually a video that he did that we used to distribute, and we call it from slave ships to ownership. So lots of young Black folks would come and talk to Griffey about how to start their own company. I would be sitting in on those meetings with him. Suge was a guy who actually had done some security work for some of the concerts that we promoted.

ALEX ROBERTS I made a momentary career change in '88. It was pro sports and entertainment. An agent I was working under had met Suge because he had many football players on his roster, and when Suge played for the Rams, they hooked up.

First time I met Suge was at a Bobby Brown concert. He approached me from behind and I knew something bigger than me was standing behind me. I turned around and I looked up. He goes, "We need to talk." I go, "But you're working right now." I surprised him. I knew he was Brown's close-protection bodyguard. I gave him my card and told him to call my office.

The next day, my assistant called freaking out, saying, "Should I call security? I don't have you down for any appointment and there's like eight guys headed toward your office."

VIRGIL ROBERTS Suge transitioned from sort of doing security to becoming a manager of different artists. So he managed Dre. He managed the DOC. And a lot of his management was just keeping these guys out of fights.

ALEX ROBERTS Suge saw an opportunity and boy, did he use that to his advantage. All of a sudden we had N.W.A hanging out in the bullpen. This was the golden triangle of Beverly Hills where Bedford and Wilshire met, and it was on the fifth floor of the Security Pacific Bank building. Just getting in that building alone through the security was tough. You can imagine guys in suits nervously riding up in the elevator with cats from South Central.

VIRGIL ROBERTS He came to the office one day and said, "Look, I'm managing this kid Chocolate. He wrote all these songs on the Vanilla Ice record, and he's not getting paid. Can you help us get paid?" We met with Chocolate and he talked about how he made these songs for Bobby van Winkle down in Texas. And so we ended up making a publishing deal for Chocolate. He got a big advance—like $400,000, because all the songs were for Vanilla Ice, the first big white rapper. So we were able to establish that, in fact, Chocolate really had written these songs. Because there was a question. I thought maybe he made it up. But we actually got a copy of a record Vanilla Ice's manager put out independently in Texas, and it gave Chocolate the credit for the songs he wrote, like "Ice Ice Baby." So there is a $400,000 advance and Suge gets 25 percent of it.*

A couple of weeks later, Suge came back with Dre. And he's like, "I've been working with Dre as his manager. He's not being paid." SOLAR didn't do rap music. I'm taking notes and I'm like, "Tell me what you did." "I did the N.W.A record that sold about a million copies. I did the JJ Fad record that sold over a million copies. The DOC record that sold a million and a half copies. I did another N.W.A record that sold over a million and a half copies. I did a Michel'le record that sold over a million." Of all these records, the only one I recognize is Michel'le, because it

*Over the years, it was rumored Suge got Chocolate credit by dangling Vanilla Ice over the side of a Los Angeles hotel balcony. In a 2013 interview on SiriusXM's *Sway in the Morning*, Vanilla Ice denied the claim: "He never hung me over no balcony. The truth is, he was nice. But the story seemed a little bit better, a little more interesting, and it got better ratings when you've got Vanilla Ice hanging upside down."

was an R & B record. I knew it had been a platinum record. So the question was: Was he telling the truth? And my initial reaction was that anyone who produced records is getting paid. I don't believe it.

Dre told the story about how he and Eazy-E were partners and the idea was that as partners, Eazy was going to run the business and Dre was going to handle the creative. But then Eazy went and partnered with Jerry Heller and next thing Dre knew, he was no longer a partner, he was just working at the company. Nobody's paying any royalties or any advances. That seemed a little strange to me. There was a lawyer who worked for Ruthless Records named Ira, and I had actually hired Ira to do some work for SOLAR. So I called him and asked him what the deal was with Dre. They had him signed as an artist because he was a member of N.W.A, but they didn't have him signed to a contract as a producer and they didn't have him signed to a publishing agreement. So Suge and DOC and Dre came back again and Griffey said, "Dre, look, son, if you can make hit records, you can make hit records. You don't have to worry about getting paid. You can just have your own company." That was really the genesis of Death Row.

Dre said anything he did he wanted to be a partner with DOC, because he did a lot of the vocal production and the writing. There was a time when it was always DOC and Dre. So he said, "I'm going to do it with DOC and Suge." So Griffey said, "Let's, the four of us, partner. I will be the senior person. You and DOC take half the company, I'll take half the company, and then we'll pay Suge as a manager fifteen percent off the top." That was the initial oral agreement. I'd actually formed a corporation for them and they said the name wasn't hard enough. They said they wanted to be Death Row Records. There actually was a trademark for Def Row—a producer named Andre Manuel had trademarked it. So I bought the trademark for, like, $25,000, if I recall.

They didn't have a lot of money, and we at SOLAR didn't have a lot of money, but what we did have was a facility. The third floor was the creative floor. That floor had a recording studio, rehearsal hall, and some meeting rooms. We turned that floor over to Death Row. And that's where *The Chronic* was recorded.

Before *The Chronic* was recorded, we had this strategy of introducing the Death Row artists to the world: we did a soundtrack to the movie *Deep Cover*. There were a bunch of Death Row artists on the soundtrack, but it was a SOLAR record. That's how I got to know Dre and Suge and DOC and Snoop—because they were in our building.

Griffey gave them that space because he knew what was being created, and he was a partner in the company they were creating. I mean, it is obvious that Dre was actually a creative genius. He had that pulse. Looking in the history of the record business, there are always people who have that sort of touch. Dre was really unique, because he was an R & B producer who could do rap music. He created a sound. That's not like the East Coast rap sound you would hear, which were just tracks that people can rap to. Dre actually created tracks that were melodies. The difference, of course, is that when you do something like "California Love," you can actually hum the music.

ALEX ROBERTS Suge approached me in 1990 and said, "Don't take this wrong, but I need a white guy to open some bigger doors." He told me, "I don't know what it is, but I would trust you with my mother." I said, "I feel the same way. Because if anything happened to me, the same would happen to you. Let's get that out of the way." We became really tight after that. He didn't push me to come work for Death Row. I knew he'd spoken to a few other people and I'd spoken to them, too, and whatever answer they were giving him they were lying, because they were telling me, "There's no fucking way. This thing is a nightmare waiting to happen. I'm getting married, I'm gonna have kids." I said, "Yeah, well, somebody's going to do it. And I'm going to dive in deep and swim."

VIRGIL ROBERTS There have been lawsuits and other things around the meeting on April 23, 1991.* Whether it happened as it's been described, I don't know. I don't doubt that there was something that took place, but for a long time "releases" were kept hidden. It wasn't like they signed and all of a sudden said, "Okay, Dre is out of this deal." That actually came about maybe months, if not a year or so, later. That's when Eazy said, "Hey, I only signed that because they threatened my life." And they probably did. If you do something under duress, it's not enforceable. But beyond all that, as a practical manner, Dre could have gotten out of his contracts, because he never got paid and never got any accounting.

Our position at SOLAR was: we ain't in it. It's something that took place between you guys, it was really designed to get Dre out of this recording agreement because they didn't have any other agreements with him. He's already free to do his publishing. In fact, just like we did a publishing deal with Chocolate, we did a publishing deal with Dre—gave him a million-dollar advance, which

*Eazy-E alleged in a 1992 lawsuit he was forced by men brandishing baseball bats—Suge Knight among them—into signing over the rights to Dr. Dre and several other Ruthless artists. The suit, seeking $54 million in damages, was dismissed in 1993.

was money they used in part to start Death Row. Because he wasn't signed as a producer, there was nothing to stop him from making records for Death Row or anybody else. It really wasn't clear that Dre really wanted to be a recording artist. He says he wants to be a recording artist, but the things that recording artists do—like make records and go out on tour—once Death Row started, he really didn't do that. On one level, it's much ado about nothing. You forced me to sign a release for the guy who is a member of N.W.A, but he didn't want to record with N.W.A, and most of the other N.W.A artists didn't want to record with N.W.A, either.

One of the things that Suge was trying to do was play the tough guy. Big guy, but he had no street cred. He was raised by his mother and father, they would send him to church on Sunday, and that's how he ended up going to college. So part of his attraction with Dre and some of the other people was, *This is a big guy who can protect me in fights. Plus, he went to college, and I didn't, so he knows more about business than I do.*

ALEX ROBERTS We got into an altercation once. A friend of mine was in trouble and I asked Suge to go in on a hard loan with me. I told him, "I've known this man a long time and he's involved in a deal. We can put in demand for escrow for our payments, but that could expose us because we can't really prove where this money came from, so it will be old school." Suge said, "Definitely." Little did I know that because I referred him, I'd get smacked, too.

Suge came into my office and said, "Where the fuck is Dean?" I guess for a second he thought maybe I was involved in shorting him. It wasn't a punch; it was like a bitch slap, and when I went to hit him back he caught my arm. It really was funny. He fucking broke down and started laughing. He said, "Are you serious?"

I said, "Sometimes you've got too much on your plate. That's what you use me for. That's what we agreed upon. That, and never for anything to go down in this office."

VIRGIL ROBERTS The studio that we built was a state-of-the-art studio. The SSL console we had was a sixty-four-track, fully computerized soundboard. The main room was big enough for an orchestra. We found the one Black sound engineer in America at Peabody Sound in Boston, and we flew him out to help design the studio. There was as much steel framing around the studio as there was steel in the rest of the building, because when you build a studio in a high-rise building, like we built, and you want the sound quality to be perfect, what you had to do was make sure that the room where you were doing the recording is isolated from the rest of the building. There were studios that were as well built, but there wasn't a better studio to work in; it was like an absolute dream sort of facility for producers.

They didn't have any money. We paid for Suge to get his car repossessed. We paid Snoop's rent. The guys who would be down in the studio, Daz and Kurupt, we would sort of take care of all of them. A lot of the SOLAR secretaries have such fond memories of the guys at Death Row because even though they were gangsta rappers, they would come up and ask them to type their lyrics and say, "You know, we don't think you're a bitch or a ho, so don't take it personal. Can you please type this for me?"

Not long after we released the *Deep Cover* soundtrack, Jimmy Iovine offered them a couple of million dollars to come and be part of Interscope. At that point in history, we had a joint-venture deal with Sony. And part of the deal with Sony was that any assets that SOLAR acquired, Sony would have a right to acquire. Dick did not want Death Row to be acquired by Sony. Therefore, his deal with Suge and Dre was on a handshake. We wanted Sony to come up with money to distribute Death Row. And that was at a point in time where all the major companies were stepping away from distributing gangsta rap. We didn't have, as a company, the money that it would take to market and promote the record. Interscope was on the verge of going out of business because they had had nothing but failure. Ted Field, who had been the financier and partner with Jimmy Iovine, had said, "I'm pulling out." Jimmy had an A & R guy that was working for him named John McClain, and McClain's father was Dick Griffey's godfather. He played *The Chronic* for John. He went to Jimmy and said, "We've got to get this record." And Jimmy said, "Whatever it takes, I'll get the record." So he went to Suge and said, "I'll give you a million dollars if you bring that record to me."

LESLIE GERARD When Tupac was in prison, he couldn't get bailed out. It was a $3 million bond and Suge Knight paid for it, and he said, "If I pay for this, I want you on my label." At that point, Tupac was on the up. He was hot; he was the guy.

VIRGIL ROBERTS Tupac had been signed to Interscope. Interscope didn't know what to do with him. Suge was really good at recognizing talent, and he recognized the talent in Tupac. He basically went to Jimmy and said, "Give me Tupac, sign his contract to me. I know what to do with it." So he then went and got Tupac out of jail and turned him into a Death Row artist.

ALEX ROBERTS It was Snoop who brought up the idea of Pac on Death Row. It's when he'd gone into Rikers on that bullshit charge. He'd been in and out of trouble already. We know how disgusting America and the boys in blue can be and how they immediately stereotype.

Suge said, "I need to ask you—because this could hurt us—do you really think Pac is innocent?"

I said, "From my lips to God's ears, yes."

"Why?"

"My experience with him. How polite he was."

WENDY DAY He came from a very poor background and never had money. So when the money started to come, he assumed that it would continue to come, and he spent accordingly. I know that 99.9 percent of rappers in the music industry think that when they have a hit record, they're going to make far more money than they do. And they do not. Unrealistic expectations led to that.

When you signed to a record label, and he was signed to Interscope, you pay everything back. It's called recouping. You pay everything back from your share, your percentage. So if they spent a million dollars on him, and he was supposed to receive eighteen points, which would be 18 percent of the retail selling price, out of every dollar that came into the company, he would be entitled to eighteen cents, but that eighteen cents would go to pay off the million-dollar marketing and advances that he received.

There were people in his life that were taking advantage of him and he knew that, and his intention was to stay down with them because he felt he owed them. They were there for him in the beginning when he had nothing, so even though he knew they were stealing from him, he wasn't going to do anything because he felt a sense of loyalty. Loyalty was extremely important to him.

GOBI RAHIMI He was highly intelligent. He was very volatile. He was very loving. He was very compassionate. And he—above all else—valued loyalty.

PUDGE THA PHAT BASTARD He stayed loyal as fuck.

WENDY DAY In some situations, he was loyal to a fault.

GOBI RAHIMI I think at one point I'd heard that he had more than forty different people who relied on him.

WENDY DAY He had loyalty to Death Row. He didn't sign just for financial reasons because at that point, he could have gone to other labels—any label would have picked him up. Part of the reason that he chose Death Row was because he felt like the East Coast was against him. It's hard for me to say this because I know how untrue it is, only because all the people that he thought had united would never ever come together. He believed that all of the powerful music influences—from Andre Harrell to Puffy, Russell Simmons to Jimmy Henchman to Haitian

Jack, like, anyone in the music industry that had power—he believed that they were a cabal. So he felt like the only way to counter that as a chess move was to sign to Death Row. Remember, when Pac was incarcerated—and I believe this was a Suge Knight chess move—[Knight] got on-stage and dissed Puffy.* I believe he did that because he was trying to pander to Tupac, and it was the perfect way to instill in a new artist your intention to ride for them. I think that that moment is what did it.

I was not excited about him signing to Death Row. There was so much drama to Death Row. There were federal agents trying to infiltrate. They always said that Suge was a gangbanger who wasn't really in the music industry, that it was trying to conceal who he was as a street mogul. Of course, I didn't know the extent of the drama or the craziness, but I was friends with guys that worked at Death Row, just like I had friends that worked at every label. And they were pretty high up in the hierarchy, and I know how stressed out they were, how frustrated they were. And I shared that with Pac without mentioning their names and without putting them in harm's way. I was pretty open with him. I said, you know, "The staff is even stressed out over there. Are you sure this is what you want to do?" And he just saw it as he had no alternatives.

I believed he could sign anywhere. I believed he could have run the price up through a bidding war; I would have happily helped him. He didn't want the help. He wanted to sign to Death Row. He was adamant about that. There were different clauses that I advised him to put into the contract; the contract was handwritten. I remember from the letters he was writing to me what was in there, and I was able to give him at least some coaching on what

*Accepting the Best Motion Picture Soundtrack statue for *Above the Rim* at the 1995 Source Awards in New York City, Knight said, "I'd like to tell Tupac to keep his guard up. We ridin' wit' him. And one other thing I'd like to say: any artist out there want to be an artist and want to stay a star, and don't want to have to worry about the executive producer tryin' to be all in the videos, all on the records, dancin', come to Death Row."

to put in there. I don't know if he ever did or not. I would like to think that he did, because he did trust my judgment and my acumen, so I hope that he did. But I sort of knew there was no choice. He was signing to Death Row.

JUSTIN TINSLEY By the fall of 1995, it was like, wait a minute, this label has Dr. Dre, Snoop Dogg, and this label has now added Tupac. We talk about super teams and big threes in the NBA; Suge had those three guys all on this label at one time. Of course, that was very short-lived: Dre left by like the spring of '96, and Dre leaving it should have been the first telltale sign, but Death Row at its peak was such a powerful example of Black entrepreneurship.

LESLIE GERARD Pac's now on Death Row. He hasn't re-leased anything yet. "California Love" wasn't out yet. He'd gotten nominated at the Grammys for "Dear Mama." I'm at a party at MCA. In walks Suge Knight with a trail of people behind him. The first person in line is Tupac. It's this kind of line of succession. Tupac sees me, jumps out, and gives me a big hug. We're just so happy. The next person in the line was Snoop. When Pac breaks from the line, everybody stops, waiting for him to get back in the line. It was like they weren't allowed to continue on until Tupac got back in front.

ALEX ROBERTS When Suge went and got him out, Pac went straight into the studio and wrote *All Eyez On Me*. For Pac to come out and do what he did . . . you would think it would've been straight to the strip club, not seeing him for a week. Then maybe, *Okay, let's get this going*. No. He made it known that we'd signed the right person.

VIRGIL ROBERTS Tupac was super talented, and what he needed was somebody to work with him on putting together his music and getting it out on the streets. Dre worked with him on his first record [with Death Row, "California Love"] and many of the other records Tupac did with a kid that had been signed to SOLAR named Johnny J.

TOMMY "D" DAUGHERTY I do remember toward the end I did maybe ten sessions for *All Eyez on Me* because they couldn't get another engineer. At Can-Am Studios they had two rooms. One in the front, one in the back. I pretty much was in the front room all the time. [Engineer] Dave Aron was in the back room. I'll never forget the day Johnny J had a box of discs that he wrote on his SP-1200. He told Pac, "Man, you wiped me out. I don't have any more beats left." Tupac had this look on his face like he was so happy. *I wiped this motherfucker out of beats.*

MOE Z MD Interscope was like, "Come to the studio, do a remix of 'Temptations.'" They're gonna drop that next. All right, cool. Did all these cool remixes and everything. And then, nope, Tupac got out of jail and was with Death Row. Not even two months later, there was "California Love." That record killed any record we did. I remember, I pulled over to the side of the road. I was blown away by how far they'd taken it.

KENDRICK WELLS Those sessions were a party going in and a party going out. It was kind of weird because you go in and you're like, *I'm at crazy-ass Death Row, the Motown of right now*, but then you get patted down by guards when you go in. Once you go in, there's all kinds of food and alcohol and respect. Music comes on and you see these beast artists step up like it's easy. They just started finger-painting all over the tracks. When you see art get expressed so easily, it's fun.

TOMMY "D" DAUGHERTY I can remember one of the Jacksons sitting there in a session, or the guys from Bell Biv DeVoe. It was amazing, the people that would show up saying they wanted to be part of Death Row. It was like, you don't even know what you're dealing with here. Death Row was about more than engineering. It was like running the whole show, like keeping the ship afloat. And if you couldn't keep it afloat, they'd throw you out the back door. And I mean, a ship with a bunch of pirates on it!

PUDGEE THA PHAT BASTARD One conversation I had with Biggie, he expressed to me very implicitly how he wished he was on Death Row, how much he did not want to be on Bad Boy [Records]. When you talk to people in their crisis moments, they're gonna tell you things that they wouldn't otherwise say. But Biggie was not happy with his situation at all. And Puffy is my guy; no disrespect to him. But it's a well-known fact, Biggie felt whatever he felt. He wanted to be down. He liked the gangster and the elevation of Pac and them, of what their movement was doing.

GREG KADING Puffy is not some gangster. He's not Tony Soprano. He was in fear for his life, and for good reason. He knew that Suge had it out for him. He knew that Suge held him responsible for the murder of Jake Robles.*

*Knight's friend and bodyguard. In September 1995, Robles was shot and killed outside Atlanta's Platinum City Club, where members of both Bad Boy and Death Row were celebrating producer Jermaine Dupri's birthday.

JUSTIN TINSLEY What really set this thing off was what happened in Atlanta in September 1995 when Big Jake was allegedly killed by Puffy's bodyguard at the time. At least before that it was just people dissing each other, but after that there was blood on the ground.

GREG KADING Jake Robles's murder—that was when blood was first spilled. Then what kind of exacerbates this whole thing is these labels starting to say that, you know, Bad Boy West and Death Row East, and that they were going to encroach on each other's territories. This just goes back to gangster mob mentality: *That's our turf.* It starts off and there's a competition. There's a rivalry. It's who can be more successful. Then you get a murder, and now it's really real. The violence is real.

ALEX ROBERTS The East Coast–West Coast thing was great for business. There was a beef but we leveraged it to sell records more than anything else. It sold one hell of a lot of records. I'd tell people to look at the positives. Just don't push it too far. And nobody needs to get shot. If you're pushing it too far, you might as well go back to the hood, and stand on a corner where you have to win every second of the day. The heat wins once and you're done. Dre—and Eazy and Cube—they'd worked so hard to get away from that life and get welcomed into Beverly Hills.

CORMEGA I was at a show in North Carolina with Mobb Deep and the people in the crowd were screaming, "Makaveli." That's the East Coast! Pac was big in New Jersey. How is it East Coast versus West Coast when this man got niggas in New Jersey, which is walking distance from New York? Big ran New York but Pac ran America.

D-SHOT He was always having fun and he was fun to be around. The women—the women loved him. One time we ended up at the, I think it was called the Freaknik, in Atlanta.* We came and he wanted to be around us. He had us come up to his room and hang around him a little bit. We hung around with him. So here's the difference: every star down there that was on TV was in that one hotel, but when Tupac came down the escalator it was a whole 'nother level. That boy, at that point, was a true superstar. He wasn't just there on no rap level; it was a superstar level—the movies and the music.

*A spring break festival in Atlanta that draws students from historically Black colleges and universities.

There were times where I don't think he really realized that, though. He was the kind of cat that would show up to yo hood by himself. He'll pull up on you. He'll have his straps on him and everything but he'll come meet you in your hood. I've seen him do it. He did that to me a couple of times. That's the kind of person he was.

PUDGEE THA PHAT BASTARD At the height of his career, with all the drama, it's looking like the Million Man March. Queens Day. He's calling me like, "I'm gonna meet you in Queens. I'm coming to Queens." I'm from the Bronx—from Harlem, but grew up in the Bronx. So I'm on my way to Queens like, *Oh, man. All right.* So I ride the train instead of driving. I'm with my brother and two friends. I'm thinking he's coming with, like, one or two people also. I get there. He calls me. He's like, "Yo, where you at?" I'm like, "I'm right here at the entrance." This is Queens Day. So everybody in the world is out. I'm like,

"How I'ma see you? There's mad people out here." He's telling me he's right there but I don't see him. So then the next thing you know, everybody that was in that park, all at once, parts like Moses parted the Red Sea. And he came walking down like he was on a runway. Basically the whole damn parade was everybody that was with him. The whole park, the whole damn Queens Day, was his people.

Publicly, he always gave me all my shine. That is what was so dope to me about Tupac. He never stopped being a fan even though we became friends and brothers. He never changed. We could have not seen each other physically in a year. It was always consistently the same energy. And for him, at this time, being this uber celebrity, to come through, tell me he's on the way to Queens. He came all the way from LA. He didn't have to hit me up. But he did, and then I get there, and the world's gone crazy.

KHALIL KAIN I was at a club in Los Angeles. I went to the bar to get some drinks. I had left the people that I was with just to, like, go to the bar, grab a drink. I got to the bar, ordered my drink. The next thing I knew there were like four women talking to me. I was chatting them up, just kind of chilling. My back was to the bar. I'm facing these women having a nice conversation. The next thing I know I see this very large Black man walking toward me—really large. He stops right behind these women, and he's like, "You're Khalil, right?" I was like, "Maybe." He's like, "I'm with Pac." As far as I knew, Pac was still in jail. "We're upstairs in a private room. We saw you walking in and Pac sent me over to come get you." All right, ladies, excuse me. I get up, I go with this man. We walk upstairs into this private room. And there's Pac with a few other people, and lo and behold, Faith Evans. Of course I'm excited. We hug and get drunk. He's busting my balls about being a failure. He's like, "What the fuck is going on? You're supposed to be a movie star by now. What are you doing?" What the fuck I want to do.

He apologized because I wrote him a letter while he was in jail that he never responded to. He's like, "Man, I saw that shit and it fucked me up. I'm trying to just do my bid and deal with them fucking knuckleheads and whatever." He looked great. His volume was on fifteen. We had a great night. He told me how much he loved me, how much he believed in me, how much he was looking forward to seeing me blow up. Tupac was a great hype man. He gave his energy in a way that you felt bigger. He was talking about signing Faith Evans to his new record label, and she was just chilling.

Seeing Pac that night gave me life. You're talking about going back to your roots, the very beginning of this journey for you. *Juice* will always be the start, the jump-off. And to see him that night, to see him at full power, that prison didn't fuck with him, it didn't sap his spirit in any way—it may have but he was not showing that. That's not what he was giving. We had a lot of fun. I planned on seeing him and hanging out. That didn't happen.

GOBI RAHIMI Tracy and I were at a pivotal point, because we were actually dealing with Dr. Dre, Ice Cube, and Tupac came into the picture, after he got out of Dannemora. He sent his assistant, Molly, up to take me up to the Malibu house that Suge Knight was renting from the assistant DA of Los Angeles, of all people. There was a water-gun fight with the Outlawz. Immediately Pac got on a call with Suge before I even got to say hi to him, and they started getting into an argument. They were arguing about money—"I'm selling millions of albums and you're giving me pennies." I was in the middle of a water-gun fight with the rest of the Outlawz and I was surrounded by them. I was holding my own and shooting them all with the water gun that Pac left on the table. And then he broke in, in the middle of the fight, and he was like, "That's what I'm talking about! That's a crazy Iranian. You outnumbered him, and he still held up." That became my moniker. He started calling me the crazy Iranian from then on. And I instantly fell in love with him. I was like, *I fucking love this guy!*

NAHSHON ANDERSON In 1996, I turned eighteen, and it was time for my high school prom. So I asked a girl who I grew up with to be my date, and she agreed. She really, really had a crush on me even though she knew that I was gay. Tupac was already there.* By the time we got there, everyone was already taking pictures with him. Once people got what they wanted and stuff, they would move on to the dance floor. By the time we got around to him, I saw him and I was just like, *Wow*, you know? I mean, that whole year, pretty much 1995 and '96, I had been playing a great deal of his music, and my cousins—everyone, really—were just crazy about Tupac. And so we got closer and closer. I remember taking pictures of him, but I don't have them anymore. But I just knew that that was going to be the only time that I would be around Tupac. I said, "Tupac, you know, hook me up, I want to work in TV and film production." He could hear me; it wasn't that loud. And he started squinting at me. He's like, "Look here." I'm thinking he's about to start rapping, but then he repeats

*Pasadena, California, high school student Tushana Howard wrote a letter to Tupac's fan club jokingly asking him to prom if he ever read the letter because her boyfriend broke up with her, and he showed up on her doorstep.

it: "Look Hear [Creations]." He was like, "That's my film company. That's doing my music videos. Look them up."

We went into the main ballroom, and we danced, and he danced with us for a while. Then he and Tushana, my high school classmate, left early. It was only Tupac, her, and Tupac's bodyguard. We had an after-party and Tupac was all anyone could talk about. In the next few weeks, I contacted Look Hear. I spoke with Tracy Robinson—my relationship was more with her than Gobi. I told them Tupac was at my prom and that I had met him and that he had referred me. I started that summer.

D-SHOT We were doing the Click album and at an LA resort shooting a music video for one of our songs. He was saying, "Hey, man, you know what, you guys come be in my video," which was "California Love"—not the *Mad Max* one, but the one he did in LA. During the weekend, we did a video for an E-40 and Too Short song in this mansion. He came to the hotel after and told us if we had time to come down to Can-Am Studios, let's make a song together.

TIM NITZ Can-Am Studios was a place that Death Row had leased for like two years—that was a studio that was like no other.

At most studios, you have to gain entry normally through an intercom; you have to go through a gate. At Can-Am, you went in through the front entrance, and it was really weird, because it kind of looked like it was in a commercial area. You feel like you're going into Joe's Plumbing and Repair. But then you go to the door, and there's like two fully suited security guards at the front, like fully armed. They pat you down—that never happened to me before in a studio—and then once you're in there, there was this constant *I gotta watch my back in here* vibe. It's a little rough in there.

There were stories of Suge Knight apparently having a big office called the Red Room. There were rumors about how this one guy, this videographer guy, did a video for them. And something went wrong and they made him go in there and drink piss. It wasn't the ideal environment for an engineer.

I remember walking into the studio; they pat me down. They opened the briefcase I had with me and everything. And then I go sit in the room and like, Nate Dogg is sitting behind me on the couch with a pistol. And I'm like, *Wow, my back's to the guy with the gun.* It was definitely a hairy studio.

D-SHOT We had a little time to kill before we had to go do what we had to do. Pulled up and hung out over there. Tupac had a 500 Benz. Suge pulled up in a red Ferrari. Of course, Suge, he's a big guy, but we some big guys, too. He had paper, and it was longer than ours, but we had paper, too. Richie Rich was there. It was a room full of young bosses in there.

Pac put his producers to work for a second and those songs wasn't working for us. So he stopped the music and he turned to me and said, "What do you want to do with this song? You tell me. Who do you want to produce it?" At the time, Mike Mosley was in there. Rick Rock, too. I said, "Let Mike Mosley do it." They got on it and then once they finished the music, Pac looked over at me again. I'm like, *Why are you messing with me?* To me,

I'm not the best dude in the building. Forty was gifted for dear life with music. I'm just rapping because I like to do it. But Pac's asking me, "Shot, what's the name of the song?" It's a whole bunch of people in there, ain't nobody saying nothing. It's quiet in there. So I just came off the top of my head with "We Ain't Hard to Find."

C-Bo was the first in the booth, hitting the gas on the microphone like he's driving a car 150 miles per hour. He hit it so hard that he upped the stakes. We all had to step up to the plate. I get on it. Forty does his thing. B does his thing, and here's this song.

Pac's IQ must have been one of the highest IQs I've ever seen. Because I sat there to see the man write his entire rap in less than two minutes. I mean, he had a blank piece of paper and wrote his part in less than two minutes. He got to be the fastest dude in the world. No wonder he made all the songs. He was quick.

TOMMY "D" DAUGHERTY What I liked about Death Row was the music was fucking the bomb. I mean, the beats were just slamming, it was real shit from the hood, it wasn't a bunch of commercial garbage.

Everything was spontaneous. Songs would happen so quickly. He'd be ready to record halfway to the studio. He was so fast it was ridiculous. His best songs he did by himself. When he had to take everybody along with him and have them do work and stuff, all that did was slow everything down. We did "Hail Mary" in fifteen minutes. Me and Lance, the other engineer, just looked at each other like, *Can you believe what just happened?* We wanted to listen to it more but he was ready to do the next song. We listened to it over and over like fifty times after he left.

He never came into the studio and said, "Let me hear the song from yesterday."

We must've recorded 125 to 150 songs. He only signed on to do three albums, which is like forty songs. He just kept going and going.

JUSTIN TINSLEY Pac's solo career was only from 1991 to 1996, and he basically spent all of 1995 in jail. His career was very short. He was such a maniacal worker that it always felt like he'd never slept. Whether he was filming a movie, whether he was making an album, whether you're doing wild stuff in the streets, it's like, *Dude, when do you sleep?*

TOMMY "D" DAUGHERTY One thing about Tupac in the studio was he was way cool. If you were down with what you were doing, he was 100 percent with you as well. He just didn't tolerate too many mistakes. He'd be like, "Do you like your job?" But if you were delivering a pizza to the studio and you said, "Tupac, man, I'd love to get on a song with you someday," he would say, "Okay, you're next in the booth." I swear to god, that's what he would say. He'd get you in there and he'd let you rap. And if you fucked up, he'd say, "Come back in six months and I'll put you on the mic again and you'll be on the song." That's how cool he was. Most artists wouldn't even let you in the room. If you look at all the people I've worked with—Paul McCartney, Michael Jackson, Prince—nobody could touch him in the studio.

MOE Z MD We were at a studio. We had just finished the one that they put out called "Sucker for Love." Originally it was called "Do for Love." We just finished that track. And it had my dude G Money, who was Radio's singer, on it. We were trying to get them out, get them going some kind of way. So we had him sing on that. After the session, Pac had this Cameo tape, and he goes, "Hey, do you think you can flip 'She's Strange'?" I told him it was no problem. He said we'd be back in that studio that Friday. I went to my homeboy's house and used his equipment because mine was broken at the time. Pac said, "This is perfect to get your brother in here to sing." My brother was doing some talent show or something and was like, "I can't do it." I'm like, "Huh??? You're doing a talent show in Carson. Tupac is asking you to come sing on a number one record!" He wouldn't do it. So Pac was mad. He said, "Go get G Money," and I had him sing the hook I wrote.

There was a kid who was on one of those competition TV shows. He ended up going solo and wanted me to do this track. So I made a track for him. A couple months go by, he was like, "My dad wants me to get the money back because I can't really do anything with the song." I came up with it and gave it back to him.

It was not even three months later that I made that cassette tape for Pac. That track was not on there as far as me putting it on there for him to hear. I was trying to tape over it. When I went to Quad, he had me looking for the beat. I played all the beats that I put on there that I knew. He was like, "No, that's not it." And then he played the cassette and I said, "Oh, that's an R & B track, man." And he said, "Well, it's a rap now, nigga."

TIM NITZ He didn't interact with the engineers that much, but this one particular session we're looping the track and we're at Can-Am. I was working with a new assistant that I did not know and who didn't really know the room that well. I asked him to hook up some gear, particularly in Tupac's vocal chain, and he didn't do it right.

Johnny J was the producer, and he's like, "Okay, Tupac is ready to start doing this vocal." So I'm getting ready to record and then I go to record them and there's no sound. So after about thirty seconds, we're going, "What's going on?" I'm trying to figure out what the issue is. And then—this is the only time I've ever seen any kind of emotion out of Tupac. He started getting agitated, like, very upset out in the studio. Then Johnny J was like, "You better get up. Like, now."

So I told the assistant to just pull the stuff he had plugged in that was going into the channel I wanted to use. The whole point was I was trying to have the assistant engineer plug in a higher-quality mic pre for his vocal. When that didn't work out, I had to go back to using the mic pre-built into the console, which was good but not the best. This is happening all in, like, a two-minute span. It was pretty gnarly. And once we're getting sound again, he's instantly calm.

GOBI RAHIMI He lost his cool a couple of times when the engineers weren't queuing up the song when he was in the booth or once when one of them turned the light off while he was in there. He would call them goat-mouthed motherfuckers. But for most of it, he was at ease.

In April 1996, he was still only three, four months out of Dannemora. It was all peace and love at that point. For "2 of Amerikaz Most Wanted," he and Snoop were straight chums. That was the follow-up to "California Love." In fact, it was a three-day shoot, and after the second day, Pac turned to me and Tracy like, "Y'all have enough for a video, me and Snoop are out." Then they just jumped in his Rolls and just mashed out.

Tracy did the physical shoot for "How Do You Want It" because I was prepping "2 of Amerikaz Most Wanted," which was shooting the week after. A guy by the name of Black was supposed to be directing that and he backed out. We got on a call with him and he's like, "I'm not doing it because I'm not sharing credit with Tupac." Because it was Pac's concept, and he wanted to be the codirector on it. I was like, "Dude, you've got Tupac and Snoop, two of the biggest artists on the planet right now, and you don't want to do the video because of a codirecting credit?!"

KENDRICK WELLS We went through this weird trip where we had just finished recording *All Eyez on Me* and he was staying at this beautiful hotel for a month. And as soon as the album was wrapped up, we got moved two hotels over to a place called the Mondrian. It was this hotel where the cats from New York stayed. I don't know why it seemed that way—like your grumpy neighbors or something. It was right by the House of Blues. It was just the weird-est thing. I remember we all sat in the room like, "What's going on?" Pac was like, "Don't worry about it; it's noth-ing." But then he told me he was sending the gun collec-tion out from Atlanta. I'm supposed to meet somebody and make this happen. Whatever Pac says, that's what I'm doing. My loyalty was with him; it wasn't with Death Row. And that caused problems for him and me. The record came out, shit went fucking double platinum the first hour or whatever. And now everybody's at ease. Tupac is in his new penthouse. It's out of the hood. No dudes are turning the corner. Suge gets wind of this gun collection—Pac tells him or whatever—and Suge tells me to go get rid of it. Which made sense because everything had calmed down.

TOMMY "D" DAUGHERTY There was one night I was drunk and I got pissed at Pac because he was doing a stupid fucking song dissing Nas. He did like five or six of them. I was like, "Dude, how many songs are you going to do this kind of shit for? You sound stupid. You could do political and social stuff for the people, not stuff for Nas." He said, "You're right, tomorrow we start the Makaveli album."* That got me excited. I'm like, "What's the Makaveli album?" Suge wanted him to do a diss album where he's dissing all the New York rappers. Instead of spending any more time on that, we switch over to do Makaveli.

GOBI RAHIMI I think the fuel on the fire was the record labels, because they're the ones that profited the most. And, you know, Suge had his own little-boy complex or whatever, flexing on who's a bigger CEO between him and P. Diddy.

TOMMY "D" DAUGHERTY Suge didn't have any respect from the Bloods and everything. They were just taking advantage of him. They didn't consider him a gang member at all.

VIRGIL ROBERTS Suge was the hunter that got captured by the game. If you're going to be the leader of thugs, you're supposed to be the baddest thug of them all. So he started playing this Humphrey Bogart role.

*The Don Killuminati: The 7 Day Theory was the final album Tupac recorded while he was alive. Released under his alias Makaveli in November 1996, two months following his death, it was his third consecutive number one on the Billboard 200 and was certified quadruple platinum by the Recording Industry Association of America in 1999.

ALEX ROBERTS Suge could get whatever he wanted from Interscope—or anybody—because people were so intimidated. What annoyed me was you have all the money, *all the money*, and you don't take care of the right things. Nobody could control him. He didn't need to be on the cover of *Vibe* magazine with Dre, Pac, and Snoop. Everything was over the top.

TOMMY "D" DAUGHERTY Death Row wasn't as fun as [Tupac] thought it was gonna be. I could just tell he wasn't digging it at all. I remember one day he picked up the phone after they sent us to some bullshit studio and he was on the phone yelling at Suge: "Why am I over here in this shitty-ass studio? People are using the good studio when I just bailed out Death Row." He was really pissed, too, because he realized he wasn't getting paid shit for what he was selling on those records.

WENDY DAY He had signed there more to protect him from the drama, and what it did was it showed that there was new drama. It got him out of one highly explosive situation into other, smaller explosive situations. It was a three-album deal. And I know for a fact that he believed he could just deliver three albums and leave. And that's not the way it works. You have to deliver three albums when you sign to a three-album deal, but there are specifications in the contract of a timeline. There were a lot of intricacies within that he just didn't really understand. When he signed it, I don't know if he really believed or just wanted to believe that he could deliver three albums and just bounce. He ended up recording something like thirty albums. A ton of bootleg albums came out after he passed, so I knew he delivered more than three. He and I hadn't spoken, but I did notice that in pictures and in videos he had stopped wearing the Death Row chain. I don't know when he stopped, but I noticed it in the summer right before he died. He started wearing an angel pendant. That was when I reached out to him to make sure everything was okay. And that's when he just fell back in step with me like we had never not spoken.

He's like, "Okay, it's time to start putting together my label. I'm going to be leaving Death Row. I've been talking to the lawyer about leaving, and I want to start shopping a deal for my company. Since I helped the East Coast and the West Coast go to war, my first project I want to put out is called *One Nation*." He had already started recording it. That was going to be the first album. I started putting the business plan together for the company. It was called Euthanasia. It had a community center program. It was sort of up in the air, but wherever it was going to be based, he wanted to make sure that we had a day care in the office. It was very foresightful, very caring. The plan was kind of amazing. He outlined it to me and then he said, "Here, you put it in writing." So I had a project, and that's what I was working on when he was shot.

KENDRICK WELLS He talked about that a little bit because when he wanted me to help run the label, he said, "Are you still in the record business?" I'm like, "Hell yeah." So I was doing my own records and stuff like that. I put my stuff on hiatus to go work with real major-label stuff or whatever. And Tupac had some ideas he wanted to work out. He knew he was doing movies, he knew he had to rap a certain way, and the way he was going to make it right was to help the young and the disenfranchised. He felt like his alternative label, Euthanasia, would fulfill something that was necessary. He was going to work with real talent. But the goal of that was to give back. It never came to fruition. So I can't say exactly what it was, but we talked about the structure of it and we talked about setting up the office and bringing Yaasmyn Fula,* and started bringing people in to set up the office and doing things to get that going, but I never saw it realized.

*A friend and coworker of Afeni Shakur who became Tupac's surrogate aunt and business manager.

ALEX ROBERTS The rumors of Pac leaving Death Row were true. He talked about it. He wanted to marry Quincy Jones's daughter.†

†Actor and model Kidada Jones, who was dating Tupac.

Quincy said to Pac, "Are you going to be able to get out clean without any trouble?" We had a meeting in New York. He said to me, "You think you'll be okay?"

I said, "We'll be okay."

Quincy asked Pac, "What do you have in your bank account?"

He said, "I don't know."

I said, "It's not what it should be and that's all I'm saying." I didn't bring it up in front of them to embarrass him. I told Pac, "I know Suge's been good to you. But by the same token, do you have anything in your name? Do you know how much money you have made?" Pac started thinking about it. He had all the watches, the gold jewelry, drove whatever he wanted. But nothing was in his name.

That hurt me because I was really close to Suge and I'd brought it up before. Nobody else would bring it up. I did it one day when we went to Fatburger.

I said, "Look, I understand business."

He'd go, "Alex, I'm doing it because we grew up differently. They're gonna take that money—whether it's one hundred grand or two hundred grand or five hundred grand—get it on a Friday, and we wouldn't see them for a week. And then they'd be calling, saying, 'Hey, I'm in Vegas and I'm broke.'"

That was his excuse for why everything was in his name. I knew better because of the look on his face.

I said, "You're doing it the wrong way. This is only going to bring more heat on you."

I told him [Suge] that Pac was no dummy. I recommended we set up a trust for each artist, so they couldn't lose anything. He told me to let him think about it. There was nothing to think about.

"I can take it and get it done this afternoon, and these guys will have a whole different level of respect for you."

His response was: "They don't respect me now?"

C'mon, man. We've made you a multimillionaire. You are untouchable and you're still playing with fire. And you're jeopardizing their careers.

COLIN WOLFE Once he hooked up with Suge and his whole camp, it was like signing a deal with the devil. I guess his ego got in the way, being that he wanted to be thug life. But I think he found after a while that, yeah, this whole thing ain't right. That's why everybody left. All of those cars and houses. None of that was in their names.

ALEX ROBERTS We owned a car dealership, West Coast Exotics, because everybody we were signing we were giving cars to. Suge said, "Never, ever register the title in their names."

COLIN WOLFE That's why I left. Because I saw how crazy it was getting, and this was right before the money started coming. Producers getting beaten up in the Red Room and all this stuff? Engineers getting beat up because they were rolling the tape back too far? Threatening your life just because you won't sign a contract? That doesn't sound like a creative environment. I had been with Dre prior to that for, what, three or four years. Through all of the N.W.A sessions, I never faced any of that. I never felt threatened.

ALEX ROBERTS Having Rampart division moonlight for us*—I mean, they were the most corrupt PD at the time, the LAPD—there were no favors done. It hurt us more than it helped.

COLIN WOLFE Tupac and Death Row felt like a great marriage at first. Until I think the business kind of got twisted. That was kind of the thing with the *Chronic* album, too. It's great at first because nobody has money. Once the money starts coming in, and then all these other people start coming in, and you're not getting your due, that starts to get to you eventually. But before that, it was great—him getting with Snoop and the Dogg Pound. They're making some great fucking records. And with the things he was personifying, he couldn't have come to a better place for production. Great place to go to get that Cali gangsta shit.

GOBI RAHIMI I directed the "Made Niggaz" video. That was one of those situations where Pac had the concept and I kind of fleshed it out for him.

*In the late 1990s, the anti-gang unit of the LAPD's Rampart division became embroiled in scandal when seventy police officers were implicated in some level of police corruption. Investigators on a task force discovered that Suge Knight hired several off-duty officers to work security.

Tracy and I fought on that one. She would over-promise the artists, and since I was sort of logistics, I knew we needed more money and more time for that video. We needed a minimum of three days. I was like, "We need four days for the video because he wants to do a short film. They want guns and scripts and explosions. We need to do this properly." She came back to me and she's like, "It has to be in two days." And so my back was up against a wall to try to make that happen.

Unfortunately, or fortunately, a fight broke out on set. And that sort of saved us. One of the stuntmen got into a fight with one of the Outlawz, and then Pac and the rest of the Outlawz jumped on top of him. I was kind of doing my best to protect the stuntman. And he was like this hard-core South Side Chicago ex-marine. He was like, "I don't give a fuck about these guys." And then when the fight broke up, he went to his car and he got a gun. And by the time he got back, they put the Outlawz and Pac in a limo and they got carted off because the video got shut down.

WENDY DAY He was always very up-front with who he was and what he did. And while he always hung around with a lot of killers, he was not a killer. He just wasn't with the rah-rah shit. And the thing about Death Row was it was entwined in rah-rah shit. He did what he had to do to feel protected. He didn't realize what he was getting into in order to be protected.

ALEX ROBERTS I knew there was some friction in the air between Dre and Pac. And I know Dre kinda had the limelight swept from underneath him. When Dre stepped away, Kurupt stepped in. Nobody really knows how good he was as a producer.

VIRGIL ROBERTS It got to the point where Dre didn't want to come around because of the people who were there. He just stopped working, stopped producing. Jimmy Iovine recognized the talent in Dre, and Dre really became sort of like the A & R guy. Eventually what Iovine did was he bought out Dre's interest in Death Row. Dre's name went on a lot of stuff that he didn't produce.

ALEX ROBERTS Those were violent, stupid days at Death Row, and every man has his cutoff point. With Dre, it was when guys started getting released from the pen. Suge's a nice guy; he's gonna want to help out his homeboys. It was a lot of, "Hey, I've got a job for you. I need a Death Row assistant." That was the thing. What does a Death Row assistant do? Hang out. Prevent whatever bullshit that could happen—but never does happen—from happening, and collect a pretty nice paycheck every two weeks. I'll never forget when too much shit went down at the studios and Dre just said, "I'm done here." Suge said, "You'll leave with nothing." He didn't care.

*Aftermath Entertainment is a record label founded in 1996 whose artists have included Eminem, 50 Cent, Kendrick Lamar, and Dr. Dre himself.

MOE Z MD Me and Shock G and Tupac's manager Atron were trying to get a record deal happening for all of us as a label, and they ended up giving the money to Dr. Dre to start Aftermath.* We had the paper on the table, sitting in the Interscope offices, and they came into the room and said, "Sorry, guys. We gave the money to Dre."

GOBI RAHIMI I remember Tupac was once going off on Suge about how a $700,000 *Gridlock'd* check went to Suge instead of him. The money conversations were happening all of the time. It felt like they were happening exponentially before Tupac died.

Suge had kept a couple of big checks from us. He had a $225,000 check, if I'm not mistaken, that was owed to us that he just wasn't paying us. And I think it was because we were Pac's production crew. And I actually went through the paperwork and realized that our contracts were with Death Row but the checks were coming from Interscope. I called up the head of legal at Interscope at the time; his name was David Cohen. "David, I think we have a little problem. I need a check." Within twenty-four hours, they sent us a check for the 225 or whatever it was.

At that point, I suggested to Tracy that it would make sense for us to own a production company with Pac because, one, he would get a piece of his own pie, but most importantly, I think Suge would have had a harder time putting the squeeze on Pac and his production company as opposed to us.

I had a DBA called 24/7 Productions. I suggested the name to Pac because he worked 24/7. Within a week, we had started the paperwork for 24/7 Productions. I think he was supposed to give us a little money for the incorporation. We were just so busy. It didn't happen. We did one video. But he literally came to us one day, and he said, "Y'all, we're gonna have a three-picture deal. Paramount, New Line, both want to fuck with me now that I'm bondable." So there were a couple of companies that wanted to mess with him. He was very comfortable with us as business partners. He ran 60 percent of the company, me and Tracy owned 40 percent of the company, and the intention was to start doing films and everything else. And he had three films that he wanted to do, and we were like, "Our lives are gonna be changed forever in the coming months."

MARK ANTHONY NEAL I knew that he was someone that was a little highly combustible. It struck me that there were other forces at play with him that impacted the way he was playing himself out publicly, whether it was the real fear on his part that there were people in his camp that he couldn't trust. Hence the whole thing that played out with him and Biggie—the East Coast–West Coast thing. We now know there were also some tensions around him and Suge Knight, what Tupac saw for himself in the future, and what Suge needed from him then. I think all that stuff kind of manifested itself out in some of the behaviors that we saw close to his death.

NAHSHON ANDERSON He did get reckless toward the end of his life, and that's understandable. That's what being shot at multiple times and convicted of certain things will do. He was angry about all of the hypocrisy, and that stuff will really just turn you into a vicious asshole.

KENDRICK WELLS When we leave the studio, the stress comes. Tupac seemed like he was always stressed out. The closer we came to the release date, the more stressed out he was. I'd never seen him smoke so much weed. And he was angry. What I realized later was he had signed his way out of prison based on what this album was going to do. So you always have doubts. You think, *Oh shit. What if this doesn't sell? What if I'm not that?* Then like one hour into it coming out you find out it's fucking double platinum. So I saw that. I saw him go from, like, being on edge to being the baddest motherfucker on the planet because he did it.

GOBI RAHIMI The House of Blues show* was on the Fourth of July and Pac was on one. He was not in a good mood. All twelve cylinders were going at the same time. He had a lot of rage. Fatal Hussein† actually walked in and, as if he was going into the OK Corral, pulled the gun out of his waistband and handed it to one of the security guards. Within two minutes, LAPD was there. They arrested him and took him away. So I think that was probably the first thing that got under Pac's skin. Then the audio guy was messing up. While Pac was getting ready to perform the song, the lineup for the songs was all off. So [the audio guy] went through five or six before he finally got to the right one, and that happened a few times during the performance. Pac was livid during that performance. There wasn't any sort of sensitivity. He was talking about Biggie and Puffy and Lil' Kim and East Coast–West Coast, and all the drama. It was just off. He was really off that day.

*Tupac's final live performance.

†Rapper and member of the Outlawz who died in 2015 in a car accident.

KENDRICK WELLS We used to have a thing called player's court, and if Tupac was your attorney, you're going to win because he's gonna say or do whatever it takes to win. He knows how people think, and he knows how to flip the script and how to make people laugh or cry.

So in the case when it comes to Death Row, they were playing games with money. I think they were doing some divide-and-conquer shit—I didn't see it that way at the time, but now I do—and he kind of backed their play. I wasn't offended by it. I realized, *Oh shit, he can't do nothing about it.* Once I saw that he couldn't have my back, I could no longer have his back. I wrote him a letter about it.

I remember the last conversation I had with him. It was right in the middle between the time I left Death Row and the time he died. We had a silent conversation. In the thickness of the silence I felt like I heard him saying, *I gotta do what I gotta do, bro.* He wasn't ashamed of me for leaving, and I wasn't ashamed of him for staying. Both acts are unvirtuous. Him staying to his end: there's no honor in that. That's not a great thing. But he did it because he felt he was honoring something. And I left because I was honoring something, because I felt like—*I'm not doing your purpose. You asked me to be here for advice. You asked me to be here to steer you right. But you're not listening.*

LESLIE GERARD Right before he went to Vegas, I was in the studio with him, chitchatting. "You know, I think I'm going to focus more on my acting career more than my music career." He said, "Suge told me that I'm worth more to him dead than alive." He mentioned something to the effect of, "I just feel like the crab trying to get out of the pot and everybody is pulling me down." There were a lot of people that started hanging around him in the studio that weren't probably the best, the right, influences. You know, that happens with a lot of people if they're not well protected.

GOBI RAHIMI Since I kind of got to be a fly on the wall and observe him, one thing that stood out for me is I think he had a tremendous amount of sadness. I would find a lot of the pictures that I took him in, he would sort of be looking down at his rings and contemplating, or in some of the footage, he sort of propped himself on a speaker with his arm, and you could just see that he was a million miles away.

CHUCK WALKER *The rebellion continued for two years. It moved south toward what is now Bolivia and got really violent. And that's when they became really close to victory. He was dead, but in 1782 to 1783 they had the Spanish on the run. The original troops from Lima are just wiped out, exhausted. They don't have any supplies. They lack basic medicine. They're suffering a great deal.*

The uprising ended with the execution of Diego Cristobal in 1783. Túpac Amaru II really tried to moderate violence. He wouldn't let them touch churches; neutral people or intermediaries were allowed to leave towns. In the second phase, it becomes almost like a caste war. Indigenous people said wearing buttons was a sign of being a European. The term that they used was actually Quechua for "redneck."

Whereas for the Spaniards, there were no more indigenous people who weren't rebels. (Despite the fact that there were, actually; the Royalists had indigenous people fighting for their sectors.) But it got really, really brutal at the end with all these horror stories, like the whole towns being executed—but also the rebels, like, burning down churches and raping nuns. A lot of this is probably exaggerated, but there's some truth to it. But afterward, the Spanish didn't go in and commit ethnic genocide. Because they couldn't. They knew that they were really close to losing. They also knew that another rebellion could happen. So there's this really tense silence afterward. If you look at the historical record, like a decade later, you almost wouldn't know it existed.

IX

GOBI RAHIMI I convinced Tracy [that we should] go to Vegas for her birthday because I knew that Pac was going,* and in my gut I felt like something was going to go wrong. She was like, "Hell no, I'm not going to Vegas," and, "Hell no, I don't want to be around Suge and Death Row for my birthday." But I convinced her. We took our production staff—that included my sister and her husband, and a few others—and we went out there.

*To attend the WBA heavyweight championship fight between Mike Tyson and Bruce Seldon, held at the MGM Grand Garden Arena on September 7, 1996.

We were at Club 662 waiting for Pac to show up when, after a couple of hours, Nate Dogg came through the crowd, came straight up to us, and said, "Pac and Suge have been shot."

RYAN D ROLLINS I was living in Suisun City when somebody told me. I was like, *This nigga keep getting shot!*

ERIC FARBER I still remember where I was the night he got shot. It was a really strange thing, because I hadn't listened to a lot. I knew it, of course, and he was such a juggernaut. And I think that my own personal politics sort of fell into paying attention to this stuff, even if I wasn't sort of a fan at the time. I went to a screenwriter's house to watch the fight. I remember thinking of him as the Black James Dean.

CATHY SCOTT I started on the political beat. I was a city hall reporter, and another reporter and I switched and I worked the police beat, as we called it there. I'd gotten a lot of sources just because you have to with a department that hides the ball. I've been to more homicide cases than I'd care to count. I knew the sergeant in homicide. You're stuck there in hurry-up-and-wait kind of moments because the coroner doesn't come right away—they don't have to because the body's there—and you get to know the cops.

I got a call in the middle of the night, at about two a.m., from one of my sources at homicide that said, "Get down to the Las Vegas Strip. Two-pack Shack-er"— that's how he pronounced it—"has been shot." I got dressed and I headed down to the Strip, and some crime-scene people were still there; all the rest of the people were mostly gone, but there were still some and it was still cordoned off.

GREG KADING A couple of Metro[politan Police Department] guys that were in a parking lot adjacent to where the intersection is, they hear shots fire out. So they go, and they see cars peeling out. They don't know who's fucking shooting whom. They see Suge make this abrupt U-turn and pull away, and so if you're seeing that type of driving, you're like, *Fuck, maybe those are the shooters.* You don't know. Nobody witnessed it from law enforcement. You don't know what your scene is. You don't know if anyone had been shot. You don't have a fucking clue. All you know is there's gunfire and cars are peeling out. *Let's go* *after that one.* There's no victim on the ground. No people screaming, "Hey, my friend's been shot."

CATHY SCOTT Two bike cops who patrolled downtown were up in the parking garage on some call and the shooting takes place. The garage is about five or six stories high and each side is wide open. So they take their bikes and haul them down. They know that it was a shooting because they heard it.

They see all the cars and everything else. They saw Suge turn around. Instead of calling for backup—because they did carry those little radios with the thing on their shoulders—and instead of leaving one of the cops at the scene, they both took off, chasing Suge Knight down the Strip as he's trying to get through traffic.

GOBI RAHIMI My gut was telling me that Suge did it.

WENDY DAY I was very nervous because I saw that he wasn't wearing the pendant, and the one thing that I knew about Suge was Suge really demanded loyalty. That was really important to him, to the point where, when Pac was killed, I genuinely thought Suge Knight had him killed. I remember calling some guys that I knew that were gangbangers that were rappers as well, and asking if that was possible. Everybody came back saying no. *Think about that: Why would you have somebody killed and you're sitting next to them?* I was just convinced that it was the smartest plan for a hit.

CATHY SCOTT He wasn't running away from the cops. He didn't know where the shooter was and he's trying to get help for Tupac. Everybody's going, "Well, why didn't he go straight to the hospital?" I don't know. He lived there. Down from the Strip, he could have been headed for Spring Mountain hospital. It was farther away than the one they ended up at—University Medical Center. But can you imagine the panic? Tupac isn't doing well. He's trying to get away from this shooter and get Tupac help. Plus he was shot. He had shrapnel in the base of his skull.

Then the cops took all the guys in the entourage and they put everybody facedown, including Suge. Put them facedown on the ground. And then they couldn't figure out why they wouldn't cooperate. Meanwhile, nobody got out to the scene of the crime for twenty minutes.

How many shell cases did people run over? How much evidence was lost? How many witnesses unaccounted for? That was a crime scene. That should have been cordoned off immediately. They didn't grab the tape from the MGM hotel right away to figure out what Tupac had been doing. They would have seen Orlando.

GREG KADING The fight at MGM Grand came about because of a preexisting incident between a gang member named Orlando Anderson, who was a member of the South Side Crips, and a guy named Trevon Lane, who was a member of Suge Knight's entourage. [Lane] had his necklace stolen [by Anderson] at the Lakewood mall [near Compton]. And so there was already conflict between these gangs. So when Trevon saw Orlando kind of hanging out loitering [after the fight], Trevon did what any person would do: he pointed it out to the guy who he's with and goes, "Hey, there's that motherfucker that robbed my chain." And Tupac took it upon himself to kind of step up and retaliate for that.

ALEX ROBERTS Pac didn't need to go after Orlando Anderson. Just let him keep the fucking chain. But there were other people around, and Suge was in sight. If they hadn't been around, Pac wouldn't have gone after him.

WENDY DAY A lot of his problems that he had in his life were due to him retaliating for other people.

CATHY SCOTT The distance from the south end of the Strip to the north end, which ends in downtown Las Vegas, is only four miles. And so the [alleged] shooters went maybe two miles and then hung a right on Flamingo. Orlando was pissed. Gangbangers don't forget, they retaliate. They're looking for him; they all know where he's going.

So they're just driving around, driving up and down Flamingo. They went down to Club 662 and waited for him. And there was a line around the block for people to get in. Can you imagine if they had come up? That would have been a bunch of people that would have been injured. That's when they were going to get him. Orlando didn't have a ticket. They came across them [on the road] and instead of having to do it at Club 662 they decided to do it there.

GREG KADING They came to Club 662 looking for them before they caught up with them later. There was an eyewitness, a guy named Mob James who was a member of Suge's entourage, and he was working security at the parking lot at the 662, and he saw the Cadillac come in and he knew who these guys were, and he knew that there had been a fight and he knew of the prior history. So of course Mob James sees these guys and the Cadillac that he knows. There are also armed officers in the parking lot, so it's not the best place if you're going to try to do a retaliation shooting.

CATHY SCOTT I got word, I think it was a hotel person who said, "Hey, you know, don't you, that Metro cops were moonlighting at Club 662?" They wear uniforms and they do conventions and stuff. But here they were at Club 662 for Suge Knight. Suge or his attorney goes to the Metro Police Department—they don't call Vegas the Little Mississippi of the West for nothing; they're not put off by wanting to hire some cops—and say, "We'd like them to be all Black."

It was eight cops and nothing happened to those guys. Well, what did they see? They were all at Club 662. Metro cops were on duty working for Suge Knight. They were on radios. What did they hear? But nobody was with them at Suge's house or to drive with them.

Some of the people in the entourage didn't have concealed carry permits for their guns. In Las Vegas you have a concealed weapon permit to carry a concealed weapon. And they were told, and they knew that. Suge lived there. David Kenner* pulled them together and said, "None of you guys can carry." Basically, he's warning them. [Tupac's bodyguard] Frank Alexander was in Kidada's car. His car was in the MGM and his gun was in his glove box. So he didn't have his gun with him. [Death Row head of security] Reggie Wright had security that only

*Death Row lawyer who, in a seeming conflict of interest, also represented Tupac. In August 1995, Tupac fired him—though as an unnamed friend told *New Yorker* writer Connie Bruck, "He didn't realize, or he refused to accept, what anyone from the street would have known—you can't fire Kenner, you don't leave Death Row."

worked for Suge. But they weren't a real security company. They weren't trained.

If you look at the Strip, the MGM was sort of between Suge's house and Club 662, so of course they wanted to make a dramatic entrance. They're out and they've got the entourage and the music's playing like crazy. So they go up the Strip to head to Club 662. They go to his house first—eat, change clothes each day—and Tupac went to the Luxor Hotel, and you can see the video of him at the valet. He's waiting for Suge to pick him up and he's hanging out with some women—of course. He tells his girlfriend, Quincy Jones's daughter, to stay in the hotel. Poor thing; she didn't go to the fight and then there's an after-party and he doesn't want her to go to that, either. She couldn't go to that party because *he* wanted to party. He was a misogynist, but she could have been killed had she been in the car. She no doubt would have been shot, because it was like a Bonnie-and-Clyde kind of thing—rat-tat-tat-tat, shoot up the side of the car.

Frank, who kept changing his story to make it better, told me that all he saw was a brown arm come out of the Cadillac from the back driver's-side seat, and then smoke, and because of all the smoke, and the firing back in the ensuing gun battle, he couldn't see a thing.

GOBI RAHIMI We called his business manager, Yaasmyn Fula, and found out that he was at University Hospital and she told us to go there and wait there until she or someone from his side showed up. When we got there Kidada and his cousin Jamala were there, and me and Tracy were the only two people from Pac's camp. We didn't trust Death Row, we didn't trust Suge, so we didn't know who to trust. It was scary. I came up scrapping, but I'd never, never been a gun dude. So I was scared shitless. But I also knew that I was the only guy there from Pac's camp that first night until the Outlawz showed up at five or six in the morning.

CATHY SCOTT I just kind of hit the ground running since I got the case so early. They put another reporter on the peripheral stories, because we were a big newspaper in Las Vegas, but by comparison to other cities we were small. We were an afternoon paper, which made the ability to do things and beat them earlier, or sometimes be late. I just delved in. We were ahead of this story almost every day.

It was all a blur at the time. I wasn't getting any sleep. It happened Saturday night. They called a news conference Sunday. I think they sent the news release out and I was told by the desk that there's a press conference at noon, or ten a.m., or whatever. It was the funniest thing to see sports channels, like ESPN, there. Homicide was just a little building that they rented. So it wasn't quite headquarters. It was in my neighborhood about a mile from my house. It was with business offices and it was unmarked.

Sergeant Kevin Manning looked like a deer caught in headlights. Never before had he seen so many reporters in his entire career. I'm sure he took questions. I'm sure they fired them off. There was quite a circle around him. He literally just had no expression on his face. I honestly think the department thought it would go away. Because, you know, this is a Black guy; this would be a Black trial.

GREG KADING Las Vegas PD knew that Orlando Anderson was the primary suspect in their murder. They knew that he had gotten into a fight with Tupac and knew that he had been involved in other violent crimes and knew that other members of the South Side Crips were in Vegas. These weren't incompetent investigators that were trying not to solve the crime.

CATHY SCOTT Orlando Anderson went home on Saturday. In the first twenty-four hours, Compton PD got the Cadillac, which went back to this auto repair shop. So they did bodywork on it and got rid of bullet holes, because Tupac's entourage shot back. CPD is saying Orlando Anderson is bragging to all of South Central that he shot Tupac. They shared that intelligence and Las Vegas cops did not do a thing.

GREG KADING When Tim Brennan* says, "Hey, the guy in the photograph that Tupac attacked, I can tell you who that is. That's Orlando Anderson. Those are some of the people that are stomping him. He's your most likely suspect," they're like, "We agree. What are you guys doing?"

Compton PD is like, "Well, as a result of what happened to Tupac, we've got a bunch of follow-up crimes, shootings, this little mini war that started, and we're gonna write search warrants, and hopefully we can come up with a murder weapon or some bona fide evidence to solidify our theory about Orlando."

The search warrants were conducted. Orlando Anderson was detained. He was detained under the premise of another murder that he was a suspect in, of a guy named Edward Webb. And so Las Vegas comes out and basically Orlando says, you know, "Am I under arrest for something?"

*Brennan and Robert Ladd were veteran members of the Compton Police Department and comprised the city's gang unit.

They're like, "Well, why would you be under arrest for something regarding us?"

So there's this little back-and-forth game. But Orlando Anderson wasn't confessing. They were strategic about how to approach him. He wanted a lawyer. And so they figured, *Well, obviously, we need evidence.* And having a cop from Compton say, "Hey, the guy on the videotape is Orlando Anderson. He's the guy that Tupac got into a fight with"—that's not evidence of a murder. That's just evidence to establish motive. But it's not evidence that you could arrest somebody and then ultimately prosecute them on. They needed corroborating witness information, and they didn't have it. Informants are saying Orlando is going around saying he did it, but that's hearsay evidence. They needed eyewitness evidence.

CATHY SCOTT The Vegas police held the case very close to their chest and wouldn't talk to Compton police. They couldn't identify Orlando, and it was the Compton police detectives who went to Vegas police and identified Orlando Anderson for them. After the beatdown at the casino, they didn't even take his name. They didn't even do an incident report. So cops show up. We can see it on video. He didn't want to file charges. They go, "Okay." It's on tape. They got it. They don't need him as a witness.

It was really a comedy of errors on their part that amounted to a really shoddy investigation into one of the biggest murder cases in Las Vegas history, including the mob. It's up there with Spilotro.* Many things would be comical, if it weren't so sad.

*Anthony "Tony the Ant" Spilotro was a mobster for the Chicago Outfit based in Las Vegas. In 1986, he and his brother Michael were beaten to death and buried in an Indiana cornfield. He inspired the character of Nicky Santoro, played by Joe Pesci, in Martin Scorsese's 1995 film *Casino*.

KENDRICK WELLS I couldn't believe what I was seeing. The first thing you think automatically is Tupac is invincible. He'll survive. Then more information started coming in.

DR. JOHN FILDES I did my general surgery training in the South Bronx. I was at the Bronx-Lebanon hospital in New York. And it's there that I developed a professional interest in treating trauma and critical care. I went and did fellowship training in Chicago, at the Cook County hospital, and was invited on faculty and practiced as faculty at Cook County trauma center for seven years. After that, I was recruited to Nevada to run and to grow the trauma center here. In 1996, it was the only trauma center in Las Vegas. Every patient injured in the city was brought to us. We always—24/7, 365, always—have a surgeon, an anesthesiologist, an operating room, and an emergency physician in the trauma center, ready to take patients out of the back of ambulances and put them on the table. Every minute of every day.

The Tupac event came not long after I started. I was at home that night, and I never saw Tupac and I never treated him. But as the director of trauma, the hospital required me to be the public spokesperson for this. That's how my name became associated with his. I personally know all the physicians who treated him in trauma and who operated on him and who cared for him in the ICU. And I've recently reached out to them for another story that was being written to see if they were ready to talk about it. And none of them will talk. At the time of 1996, they were afraid for their personal safety and the safety of their families because of the uncertain circumstances surrounding this. And now they're concerned about the federal regulations for patient protection. The statute of limitations on that's not until thirty years. So nobody will come forward who actually touched or treated him, but I was a public spokesperson. I know everything that went on about it, and I can talk about it.

On a night like this, we would receive a radio call from EMS saying, "We're inbound with a patient with multiple gunshot wounds and unstable vital signs." And we would assemble the trauma team around in the trauma center. They would be wearing operating gear like hats and masks and gloves and gowns, and they would be standing around the gurney waiting for the patient to arrive. So they're ready. It's go time.

We had an anesthesiologist, we had a surgeon, we had an emergency medicine physician. We had resident physicians, nurses, technicians from respiratory, from laboratory, and so forth. He was one of two patients who arrived. The other patient was far more stable. He [Tupac] had low blood pressure and was treated with IV fluids and blood and immediately prepped for the OR. He also was intubated and artificially ventilated. There are photos of him on the ventilator. He went to the operating room, and he had lifesaving surgery and then was taken to the ICU and was managed minute by minute, twenty-four hours a day.

A lot of the physicians didn't know who he was when he came in. And I mean, when we work on a Friday or Saturday night, we get people coming in one after another after another, and we don't get their names. They didn't realize until later that evening, or till the next day, that Tupac was of importance to the media and the arts. So he was treated cutting-edge, he was treated aggressively, and he was treated well, like every other patient gets treated when they come through the door. They didn't really engage him as a celebrity.

GOBI RAHIMI The first night they had him on the first floor and he was visible from outside the windows. Yaasmyn tried to get them to move him, but they weren't having it. I felt like I was Enzo the Baker, the Persian version. It was unreal. It was the number one rapper in the world and it became so clear that a Black man didn't "deserve" what white people did.

It was just a very eerie reality. On the third day, the marketing director walked up and was like, "They're going to come finish him off. They just called the Row, they're coming." That's when I called Vegas PD to get them to send troops. I called the cops to try to get the cops to come to the hospital and they were like, "Should something happen, there's a foot patrolman in the hospital. We're a little understaffed right now." The security guard started laughing. He told me there was a rodeo star that had broken a leg the year before; they gave him four policemen around the clock and six honey wagons for his family to be comfortable.

CATHY SCOTT It was confusing during that week, and the weeks to follow, because we were not getting the facts straight from the police. So I talked to Compton PD almost immediately and then found out that they had intelligence from the street. Then I go back to the [Vegas] police and say, "Well, this is what I know." *No, we don't know about that. No, we're not in touch with them. No, it was unrelated.* It almost felt like a cover-up at the time.

GOBI RAHIMI Pac was in an induced coma almost the entire time that he was out of surgery. I sort of volunteered for the twelve-to-eight-in-the-morning shift at the hospital, because it just didn't seem like anyone was there protecting him during that time. They had posted up a Death Row guy, but you know, I didn't trust them. Each night, it would be me inside the ER waiting room—I figured I'd be the last line of defense—and then one or two of the Outlawz would be outside, posted up in the car, and, after the fact, I learned that they had gats with them, and they were ready to blast anyone who came in.

DR. JOHN FILDES I was briefed that on the night of the injury there were a significant number of very, very concerned people who came to the hospital. I was briefed that helping them deal with this unexpected injury, and de-escalating any emotional or angry feelings that they had, was a central part of the evening. If you look in the *Las Vegas Review-Journal*, they actually have photos of candlelight vigils being held outside the trauma center.

CATHY SCOTT The trauma unit was at the emergency entrance to the rear of the hospital. It was lined with cars. They'd stand on top of the rooftops, his music would be blaring, and they'd have boom boxes. A lot of people came, but it was mostly Black people from the west side paying their respects and trying to figure out if it was okay, hanging outside. They'd watch when a doctor would come out and talk to the media.

DR. JOHN FILDES I would tell you that that level of media attention is not uncommon for people who practice in the area of trauma. I made myself available daily, and as often as required to discuss his conditions. So there really was, from our side, we went out of our way to create a flow of information that was appropriate for the circumstance.

GOBI RAHIMI This fat white nurse will come out and give me progress reports. And I think it was the second night or third night she came out, and she said, you know, "That Pac of yours is a fighter." She said, "We've had to put him in an induced coma because each time he comes to he tries to pull those plugs out and get out of bed." She said when you're a gunshot victim, when you become conscious, you wake up at the scene of the crime.

I didn't go in and see him, for whatever reason, until the fifth night. The same nurse finally came to me like, "Baby, you've been sitting here all these nights, how come you haven't gone to spend some time with him?" And so I got up and went in. It was a horrific sight. His head was twice the size of normal; I guess he had water on the brain. It was just cloaked with a sheet, and everywhere that he had a bullet wound had a patch of gauze. I went up and put my hand on his arm, said a little prayer, and walked out.

CATHY SCOTT The trauma unit always had a uniformed guard inside its lobby. Afeni had said that she would be the one to decide who could go and visit, and even Kidada couldn't go in whenever she wanted to. He was in grave condition. His body crashed during the week and they did surgery.

GOBI RAHIMI So I'd heard that his pops* was coming into town, and he came into town straight to the hospital

*Billy Garland, a man Afeni Shakur referred to in a 1997 *People* magazine interview as a "gold digger" and the "designated sperm donor." Tupac had assumed he was dead until Garland visited him at Bellevue Hospital following the 1994 Quad Studios shooting. "After I got shot, I looked up, there was this nigga that looked just like me," he told Kevin Powell in a 1996 *Vibe* interview. "And he was my father. That's when I found out."

with his luggage. He didn't have a place to stay. At that point—the third night or the fourth night—Tracy had left. Tracy couldn't take it anymore. She asked me to come back to LA with her. I was like, "No, I'm staying." She sort of had a meltdown. And every so often she would go into this, "My people, my people, they kill themselves, they're killing each other." And she bounced.

So I had a room with the hospital, and since I was doing the graveyard shift, I was like, you know, "I'll take you, Billy, and you can kind of stay in my room, at least for the night." That same day, Kevin Hackie* came into town. He was all wigged out because Vegas PD had stopped him in the airport, and then took his gun and his badge and said he didn't have any jurisdiction in Vegas. So he's all wigged out as to how they knew he was going to be there. He needed a place to stay, so I sort of put the two of them in the room together.

I've heard varying accounts on his credibility, but he sort of divulged to us that he was an undercover FBI agent at that point. Then he whipped out a card and he said, "I'm working on a case against Suge and Death Row for money laundering and drug racketeering," or something like that.

DR. JOHN FILDES The kind of gunshot wound that he had is immediately fatal for most people, and for those people who survive the surgery—a surgery that required removal of a lung—80 percent of them don't survive. Those are the precise numbers from the literature.

CATHY SCOTT There was a sense of not knowing, and there was a sense of worry, but there was also a sense

*Former Tupac bodyguard and FBI informant.

of hope that he was still alive and he was going to make it. You have to make it past the seventh day. He made it past the first. And the third is bad, especially for a chest injury—he passed that. And I talked to a doctor who said the seventh day is another integral moment. If you make it past that, then he's got a chance.

MARK ANTHONY NEAL The thing that I remember most about the shooting—and a lot of folks who were paying attention at the time, it surprised no one that, you know, he stayed alive for another week. It was just something about his spirit and his nature. We talked about him, you know, broadly, as kind of a warrior. It wasn't a surprise that he fought to stay alive for so long.

DR. JOHN FILDES In the pathology reports, and the coroner's reports, which were leaked, it says that he had a gunshot wound through the pulmonary hilum. It's nearly immediately fatal in more than 90 percent of people, and [among] the small number who survive surgery, 80 percent of the patients who undergo pneumonectomy die. It's a bad injury. The fact that he got off the OR table and our critical care teams, through some very sophisticated ventilator strategies, and some very careful cardiac strategies, were able to bridge him for several days . . . He survived that injury better than any other patient in my thirty-year career.

CATHY SCOTT But they couldn't stop the bleeding in his chest, and that's what killed him. It just kept ripping open.

DR. LEON PACHTER All the people that I knew, the guys that look to him for their rap music in the hospital, say,

"Oh, you think if he was here, you could have saved him?" I said, "You know, maybe? I don't know."

In New York, I think he was shot by a .22; I remember that it was a lower-caliber bullet. If it had been a .45 or a nine-millimeter, or even something bigger than that, he would have had major, major injury. The report said it was like a twelve-doctor team; a lot of that is hyperbole. It could be a team of about four, five, six; I don't know about twelve.

DR. JOHN FILDES Now, there were a lot of people who wanted to have a philosophical discussion or get into a series of what-ifs, which really is not productive. And those people may have been disappointed. There was a desire for a lot of people to get into hypotheticals. I would say, "He's in stable but critical condition," and people would interpret "stable" as "He's going to be fine." I can't help how people interpret the information when the information is given in a very clinical and accurate way. So you can only imagine all of the terrible things that you'll see on the news that affect individuals anywhere, and the emotions and the desire for a favorable outcome temper how people think, speak, and interpret things.

He was very unstable. The clinical course of a patient who was forced to have a lung removed as a lifesaving measure after trauma is a fairly predictable pathway. And that pathway leads to poor pulmonary function, and eventually, heart failure. It's a well-documented course. He was young and strong, so he lasted longer than most. The same words I'm saying to you were said to the family. I painstakingly presented all the information, to be fair to Tupac and fair to them.

CATHY SCOTT That last day, you could just tell by the hospital staff what had happened. I remember one of his young backup singers came out and then just collapsed on the curb and just sobbed. Kevin Powell looked like he'd just lost his best friend. Nobody talked. Nobody was talking to each other. But you could hear his music playing from the street.

RYAN D ROLLINS Days passed, and then somebody close to the situation called me and told me that he'd died that morning, and then it came on Channel 2 news immediately afterward. I remember thinking it was weird. I just knew in a minute we were gonna hook back up. I'd come down to Hollywood or wherever he was. I was still getting messages from him every now and then. I was just like, *Wow, it's over that quick.*

CATHY SCOTT When he died, I was at the hospital. Like two weeks earlier, the *Las Vegas Sun* had just launched its website. The *Las Vegas Review-Journal* did not [have one]. I think one or two TV stations had websites coming out. We were up and running, not knowing this was going to happen. So I was at the hospital with my radio that went straight to the newsroom and to the news desk, and Tupac was pronounced dead while I was there. Kevin Powell was there, too. He looked like the whole world had just ended. There's a video of me where Suge Knight is walking past me. And he's going into the trauma center because he had been told to get to the hospital. And when he got there, it was too late. We waited and waited. We knew it was coming, so I was writing the story. I was interviewing people—I got a comment from the hospital—and I was just waiting for the final word. And I phoned it in to the news desk. We were the first to report his death. The hits on the website shut it down.

KHALIL KAIN I was on this show called *Lush Life*—it was me and Lori Petty, Karyn Parsons, and John Ortiz; it lasted like six episodes—when Pac passed. And Lori Petty was the one who told me, because he was in the hospital. I was always of the attitude telling everybody, like, "Fuck, it's fine, man. Apparently bullets don't bother him."

I was on my mark. We were setting up a closer. It was a Halloween episode that we were shooting. Lori came up from behind the camera and she was like, "Your boy just died." I was like . . . *What?* "I just heard on the news: Pac just passed away." We were on the Warner Bros. lot, on the soundstage. I walked right off the set. I sat down outside the door on the soundstage and just cried my eyes out. When that happens, you understand that that whole period of your life has been marked.

CATHY SCOTT One of the best things I did that first week was I knew from the police and from the mortuary that his body was taken from the morgue rather quickly to the mortuary from the coroner's office, which meant his coroner's report was complete. I just walked into the coroner's office. And they've always recognized me from the paper, and I said, "I'm looking for the coroner's report on Lesane Crooks." By that point it was on the news release but I did not say "Tupac." I did it purposely. His mother never legally changed it.

The woman handed me the report for a $5 fee and

then I got back to the newsroom. It was just some clerk at the front desk. And I'm holding my breath the entire time. Because I was just dying to get more information from the report to say what killed him, where he was shot. I was not getting very good stuff. The hospital was kind of spotty. I was in the newsroom for about five minutes when she called me back and said, "We made a mistake. I shouldn't have given that to you, because it's an open investigation. Would you return it?"

I said, "I'm sorry, I can't." I got that autopsy report almost immediately, because I knew the police were just shutting down everything.

Tupac was the underdog. He was the victim. It's a shame that he died the way he did and the police department didn't care enough to try to solve it.

GREG KADING In 2006, the city of Los Angeles is facing a civil lawsuit, which was based on some claims that there were rogue LAPD cops involved in the murder of Biggie Smalls. And then there was a comprehensive cover-up to protect those rogue cops. So those are the allegations that led to the lawsuit that led to a reinvestigation of Biggie's murder.

Well, that's how it all started, with Biggie and trying to figure out what actually happened with him and whether any of these allegations were true. And then, you know, we always knew that there was a likely connection back to Tupac, because that just made instinctive sense. From September 1996, there was always kind of collaboration and sharing of information between Las Vegas and Compton, Las Vegas and LAPD, and anything that they thought was potentially relevant to their homicide investigation out there in Nevada. So there was a lot of sharing information back in those early days.

When I got involved in 2006, we already had all of that material, we knew what information had been shared, what different approaches they took in their investigation, what Las Vegas thought, and that there will always be some common denominator at some point between the murders.

We ultimately stumble upon a guy named Keefe D who is a Crip that we knew was associated with Bad Boy. We also knew that he was there that night Biggie was killed. There were claims that he had been doing security for Bad Boy, and that there was an outstanding debt owed to him and his crew. And then perhaps Biggie's murder was in retaliation for that unpaid debt. He was a person of interest, if not a suspect.

We also knew that Orlando Anderson, Keefe D's nephew, had gotten into a fight with Tupac in Las Vegas. So he had the motive and the means to kill Pac. So that was the most obvious explanation for Pac's murder. Once we get Keefe D in an interview room—and we've got him under very compelling circumstances, where it's in his best interest to tell the truth—he revealed that, "Hey, I can't tell you anything about Biggie's murder, because we didn't do it, but I can tell you about what happened to Pac, because we did do that."

When Mark Anthony Bell was beat up,* the person in his face in that assault was Tupac. "Tell us where that bitch lives, motherfucker, we'll beat your ass." That was Pac. So when Mark Anthony Bell goes and tells Puffy, "Man, these

*Allegedly, at a 1995 Death Row Christmas party, Bell, a record promoter, was beaten and made to drink urine in order to force him to divulge Puffy's home address. Bell did not press charges and received a $600,000 settlement from Death Row.

dudes are after you and they're after you bad, and Pac is all down for it . . . ," [Puffy] knew that Suge had kidnapped a guy and was basically threatening to kill him if he didn't tell Suge and his goons where Puffy lived. Puffy was legitimately in fear for his life, and he realized that if you come to LA, you got a target on your back, and, you know, you either do a preemptive strike or you suffer the consequences of getting caught slipping.

His first step was, *Well, I just got to get some people around me that I feel can be my first line of defense should Suge and his crew come snooping around. I need guys like [Suge].* So he gets some Crips. It just so happened by mere fortuitous fate that he was very close to this guy named Zip, who was a Harlem dope dealer. He was getting his dope from a Crip out in Los Angeles named Keefe D. So when Puffy started to complain to Zip about his problems, saying, "LA is a problem. Suge's a problem. I got problems. What can you do?" Zip says, "I got the answers for you, I'll hook you up. My boy, when you go to video shoots or you're out in Los Angeles and you feel vulnerable, his people can be your first line of defense." His mindset was, *I'm gonna get people around here that understand these dynamics.*

I think it was out of desperation and fear. After Mark Anthony Bell was kidnapped and accosted, [Puffy] told Keefe D, "Man, this is getting serious. Anything you can do to eliminate this problem for me, man, take care of it." Well, that means a particular thing to a guy like Keefe D. Puffy's just talking out of fear—"I need these motherfuckers out of my life." I don't think he's thinking, *Okay, listen, I want to have a contractual agreement that I'm going to pay you a certain amount of money, and then I want these guys killed. Do you understand? It's something much more nuanced.*

CATHY SCOTT I think because of the way the police department acted, they didn't bring out all the facts for the media and we all had to chase it down and figure it all out on our own—except for Compton PD, they were straightforward. I think that [the Las Vegas police] are partly responsible for all the conspiracy theories surrounding the case, because they didn't just come straight out and say what happened. It was as if they didn't care enough to solve it. If it had been a white rapper, if it had been Eminem, or if it had been a white singer who did a different genre of music, they would have solved the crime. They just looked at him as a thug.

Say there's a shoot-out on the west side—or in any other city. There's a shoot-out and two Black guys shoot each other. Cops call those a twofer. They don't solve those unless you've got some really good gang cops. They should have put the gang cops in Vegas on it, and they could have worked with the PD in Compton and brought charges against Orlando Anderson.

GREG KADING We became aware of the white Cadillac and Terrence Brown*, whose mother-in-law rented the Cadillac. So there's a connection, because we knew T. Brown and Keefe D and Orlando and all that were very close. We had good reason to believe that T. Brown had been in Las Vegas, and we had good information that the other guy in the car, DeAndre Smith, was in Las Vegas. Both were doing the same thing as Orlando, which was running

*Allegedly the driver of the Cadillac from which Tupac was shot, Brown was shot and killed in a 2015 Los Angeles double murder.

around telling people in their crew that they had done the murder. It's information from the streets. It's of value in the sense that it's corroborating your suspicions. But it's not prosecution evidence.

CATHY SCOTT They could easily just name Orlando Anderson as the killer, close that case. They won't do it. It's almost like it is stubbornness on their part. Because all the evidence points to it.

GREG KADING We have a tendency of forgetting that this is twenty-five years later. This plays out in a very slow, almost perfect storm for it not to be solved. First of all, nobody's cooperating. Nobody in the entourage, nobody that knew that it was the South Side Crips, was coming forward and going, "Hey, I saw Keefe D in the parking lot right before the shooting in a white Cadillac." Nobody's talking to the cops about that. They're not getting any of that information; that didn't come until long after, a decade later. They're sticking to the street code.

CATHY SCOTT Everybody who was in the car that night, they're all dead—except for Keefe D, if he was in the car; I was never told that Keefe D was in the car until later. One of those guys ended up dead in that bloodbath during the days when Tupac was alive.* That's when some of the people who were in the car got killed, and that's really where justice was meted out.

GREG KADING Of course, in 1998, Orlando died.† Until we got involved almost thirteen years later, we didn't even actually know exactly who was in the car. And nearly

*In the days before Tupac died, gang warfare erupted in Compton between the factions on either side of the shooting. Drive-bys left three dead and twelve injured. Darnell Brim, a leader of the South Side Crips who was alleged at one point to be one of the men in the Cadillac, was killed in one of the subsequent shoot-outs.

†Orlando Anderson was killed along with two other men in a May 1998 drive-by shooting.

everybody in there has died, like universal karma. Orlando died in the exact same way that he should have died; like, perfect justice.

KENDRICK WELLS I recorded some footage for a song called "Unconditional Love." It was originally entitled "Things Change." Tupac went ahead and called Johnny J and told him to meet him at a certain time. Tupac went to Tower Records and grabbed this sample. And Johnny J hooked that shit up, like, instantly. They brought in a bass player, a guitar player, and a keyboard player in the making of this song. Johnny J and Tupac are bantering back and forth, having fun, laughing, and, you know, recently I was looking at footage, and it was like that was the last of the peaceful times. They're all having fun. I look at this video and I'm like, *Damn, four dudes in this video are dead.*

STELLA NAIR *One of the things that I think is really important to emphasize is how important Túpac Amaru II is to indigenous people today. It's very common to see the motif of the execution of Túpac Amaru on most of the textiles in the Cusco area. Everybody knows about him in the indigenous communities, and you'll find his representation in a lot of different arts. And what's interesting to me is that the way that he's remembered is the execution. Most commonly, he's being quartered. It's the moment when his limbs are tied to horses and his body's being ripped apart. That's a really powerful statement that elicits anger.*

Today—and I speak from the community that I have been working with—he's seen as an inheritor of the Inca. And I think that's a really powerful statement because it acknowledges that indigenous people and individual indigenous community identity don't end with the arrival of Europeans. That resistance doesn't end, and that alone is just a really powerful movement in history to remember. He symbolizes so much about that continuity to the longer path and the counternarrative to "The Europeans came and everything crumbled." Everything he represents goes against all those different misconceptions.

X

BARBARA OWENS He was reading the third act in *Othello*, where he was about to snuff her out with the pillow. He got through the scene and I stopped him and said to all the class, "You will never, ever hear or experience a reading of *Othello* like this ever again in your life. Remember this moment." And I was thinking, *Did they remember that moment when they learned that he died? Did they remember that moment?* Because it felt like a hole in my gut. It's a different kind of knowing of that person. Sometimes it isn't personal. But it's still a rather intimate kind of knowing.

DR. JOHN FILDES I can say that the physicians who cared for him were really changed forever.

MARK ANTHONY NEAL I was teaching my first semester at the University of New Orleans. In the fall of '96, it was my first tenure-track gig. The thing that I couldn't appreciate at the time, that quickly became something that I paid attention to: I'm teaching, you know, seventeen-, eighteen-, nineteen-year-old students, who for the most part were about ten years younger than I was, and their connection with Tupac was very different than mine. And the way that they were reacting, the mourning that ensued, it was the thing that stayed with me for a long time.

TIM NITZ I teach at the LA Recording School. I do have a fair amount of students who were born after he passed away. And of all the people that I talked about, or that they find out that I've worked with, Tupac is the one that they care about.

RICHARD PILCHER Some years after Tupac died, I took a sort of sabbatical for a year and taught at an American school in England. We had a number of international students, particularly one summer: it was students from all over the world—Saudi Arabia, Italy, you name it. And I didn't particularly talk about Tupac, but the word got out. Kids came up and talked to me, and I don't want to be blasphemous, but it was like I was a disciple of Jesus or something. With awe in their voices: "You taught Tupac?!" Yeah. "Oh my god, what was he like? Tell me anything you can tell me."

We would have dorm checks and I would go into the students' rooms. I remember this one, I guess he was fourteen and small for his age, white male. I want to say he was from Italy, but I could be wrong. And there were posters of Tupac on practically every inch of wall space. I realized then what an international phenomenon Tupac was. I had no concept until these kids would just flock around me. I was sort of stunned. I suppose it's the same as if I taught Elvis or John Lennon. It was that kind of awe it inspired, and it felt weird, you know? He was a kid, a nice guy, I taught him, go away. But that was kind of a revelation for me. I hadn't really gotten it until that point.

CATHY SCOTT People couldn't quite imagine someone as full of life as Tupac dying. He'd light up a room. He was like Obama. Full of charisma, like Kennedy. He was like the next Malcolm X. People can't wrap their brains around that. One day he's here, the next day he's gone; they can't accept it. Even new generations: I taught at UNLV and it was like, "He's alive, right?" Well, no, he's still dead.

CORMEGA You know something different is happening when people don't even want to accept that they're dead. When they said Biggie was dead, we were sad. When they said Jam Master Jay was dead, we were sad. When they said Big L was dead, or Pun, or Prodigy . . . But when they said Pac was dead, people didn't want to accept it. It just goes to show you the impact that he had.

MARK ANTHONY NEAL The hologram at Coachella* was just eerie, more so than, like, the Michael Jackson example and whoever else got re-created. It was eerie with Tupac, because since Tupac died, there has always been this uneasy feeling that Tupac wasn't gone. All the rumors about him in Cuba.[†] The fact that there was a video[‡] depicting him entering heaven being released two days after he died. The fact that there was so much music released after his death.

TIM NITZ He had done so many songs that a substantial amount of music came out after the fact, after he passed away. But I think due to legal issues with his mom and Death Row and all that stuff, nothing ever really panned out.

*At the 2012 Coachella Valley Arts and Music Festival, Dr. Dre and Snoop Dogg performed alongside a two-dimensional projection of Tupac.

[†]Among the many conspiracy theories surrounding Tupac's murder is that he faked his death and went into hiding in Cuba.

[‡]"I Ain't Mad at Cha," the final single off *All Eyez on Me*.

ERIC FARBER There was a lot of unreleased music that was floating around. And so people as far away as Australia had been able to get ahold of this stuff. They were putting albums together. A lot of people were remixing songs and putting those out. One of the duties that I was tasked with, especially early on, was going after websites and going after places that were illegally distributing his content. It wasn't super early in the days of the internet but early enough that nobody had really sort of gone around and collected the domain names and things like that. Interestingly enough, there was a lot of stuff that was pretty groundbreaking in the legal things that we did on behalf of the Tupac estate. eBay was selling all sorts of merchandise that was knockoff merchandise. Nobody had really gone after them for trademark infringement for sort of acting as a middleman. So we were early in talks with eBay, way back when, on setting up a program to be able to have them pull illegal stuff. There was a lot of stuff that we actually did in the early days of internet commerce. We sued Amazon, too. Afeni Shakur was the executor of the estate and she was a fighter. She had been a fighter her whole life.

There were so many buyers; it was pretty insane. There were thousands of websites that I went after, for various things. In the early days, they used to have this process called the ICANN; it was a dispute resolution process. People really weren't happy about it. There's some song out there by some obscure rapper who's, like, killing me in a song. I got this nickname as the Thug Lawyer. People didn't like that the lawyers had sort of stepped in. Because it was such a massive fan base that felt very entitled.

KENDRICK WELLS We did stuff in San Francisco that didn't come out until he died. We recorded so many tracks at so many different studios and would've expected all of them to be hits because that night—two or three a.m.—you're listening to this stuff and you're like, *This is genius.* But it never came out. Once the estate remixed all the stuff and it started coming out, I started realizing what it was: he wasn't talking about shooting people; he was talking about the Black struggle. But that stuff didn't make it to records. Interscope didn't let that stuff out. They wanted the opposite.

It wasn't until, like, a few years after he died and I started hearing these remixes that I'm like, *Why didn't they ever play any of this shit while he was alive?* I didn't notice the difference. I wasn't mature enough yet to notice the shit he wrote at the beginning versus the stuff he was making toward the end. On the *Killuminati* album, he was awake and spiritual. But the *All Eyez on Me* shit was just a gangsta party—"Look at me, motherfuckers, y'all tried to hold me down but look at me now." It was all brilliant shit. I was right there for almost every song that was recorded. And it felt good doing it. But it wasn't until later, when they started releasing the stuff that I saw him record when we were coming up, that I could see the difference. They wanted destruction over creation.

NAHSHON ANDERSON It wasn't until I got much older that I started to realize. I was like, *Wait a minute: Tupac was at my prom, I got my start working in the TV and film industry because of his internship.* That internship opened up all these other doors for me. I would go into some of the Tupac Facebook groups and post about that, and

I'd have all these messages from people in Africa talking about how much they love Tupac. I didn't really respond to them because it was so many of them. I'm just saying to myself, like, *All I did was go to my prom and he was there.* I didn't know him. I was just a fan who just happened to be at the right place at the right time and got lucky.

MARK ANTHONY NEAL In 2003, Harvard hosted a talk called "All Eyez on Me: Tupac Shakur and the Search for the Modern Folk Hero." As far as I know, it was the first of its kind. It was something that was pulled together by Marcyliena Morgan, who had just established a hip-hop archive at Harvard. And this is really one of the first big events that the archive did. And she was able to draw in so many different folks who had different kinds of impressions of Tupac—whether we were talking about someone like Michael Eric Dyson, who had just published a Tupac book [*Holler If You Hear Me*] two years earlier, or folks talking about him in the context of stage and theater and visual arts internationally. In retrospect, I don't think there was another singular figure in hip-hop, at that time, that could have brought together the range of people that were brought together there.

This was the thing about Tupac: However you felt about his music, or his flow, his technical abilities as an artist, he had that thing, the thing that you can't teach. He was destined to become an icon of that moment. At that point in time, there were no figures in hip-hop like Tupac, dead or alive, that resonated in that way.

The thing that I appreciated about the symposium, and Dyson's book also, was when I got more of a backstory of who he was, to find out that he was such a voracious reader. And how there were young folks who would read books about Tupac and then go out and read the books that Tupac was reading. In a culture in which we almost accept the fact that young Black men don't read—that young Black men *can't* read—he almost becomes this portal, you know, to a reading life for your Black man.

SHARONDA DAVILA-IRVING Growing up in the Panthers, you're not gonna not read, because that's how you learn, and learning was important. And in order for Black people to be liberated, you had to read and understand what was happening around you.

JANE RHODES Young people are looking for models. I'm a college professor. I've been teaching some version of Black studies for almost thirty years. And every decade, the Panthers are always this model for a kind of radical Black resistance. As new generations emerge, they're looking around. Are they going to look to Barack Obama? No. They go to the media icons, the celebrity Black militants. I think Tupac continues to play a role in making the Panthers resonant.

BLU There is a small number of huge organizations that really drive our culture. The Black Panthers, the Nation of Islam, and such. Tupac represented the Black Panthers in hip-hop. He seemed to be one person carrying this massive load on his back. It's unbelievable. He was proud to carry that burden. He never put it down.

NAHSHON ANDERSON The fact that he was able to articulate the experience of so many young Black males who are victims of violence, victims of police brutality, racism, all of the social ills that, you know, we're forced to deal with . . . He seemed really, really sincere. I think about what's going on now, and listening to some of the stuff he was talking about twenty years ago and is still so relevant now, I can't imagine what he *wouldn't* have been doing.

GOBI RAHIMI I think he was the cocoon that was working on becoming a butterfly. I think he was maturing; I think he would have eclipsed the P. Diddys and Jay-Zs, not only in abundance, but in the body of work that he would have created. I also think that he would have probably dabbled in politics or social issues, because that was important to him. I think he knew that he had a responsibility, and I think he would have been a lot more useful to not only his own people, but to all disenfranchised people of the future. In his last days, I saw more calm and respect out of him for the people around him.

KHALIL KAIN I feel like Pac had a very vivid understanding of what he had to offer. I feel like the world was catching up to him. He wasn't coming into his own. He already owned it. He just needed the right vehicle. And if his schedule permitted, he was more than willing to go and do that movie, or do that TV show, or to do that play. I would have loved to see Pac onstage. And I'm sure that would have been something he would have done in time with maturity and availability and just the freedom to kind of explore.

LEVY LEE SIMON The world lost so much when he passed. I saw his future: sky's the limit. The way his trajectory was going, he would have been an award-winning, Oscar-winning actor or something like that. He had it. He had the gift.

KENDRICK WELLS I think he was going more toward the movies.

GOBI RAHIMI For the "Made Niggaz" video, there was a DP by the name of Matty Libatique, who went on to do Darren Aronofsky's films, the first two *Iron Man* films, *A Star Is Born*. He's become a huge DP.

We were doing a setup, and there was a table in the main room, while they're sort of strategizing how to take over this Piggy and Buffy drug operation in LA. And it was a lit table. I asked Matty to put the camera on the table, but I told him instead of him operating, I wanted him to reverse the handle so it was next to the lens. So Pac or the Outlawz would actually be operating the camera for the single take of the "Made Niggaz" video called the 360.

And you can see the way he moves with the camera, the way he moves in and out of frame—it's just poetic.

KENDRICK WELLS He had scripts. He had two movies coming out that hadn't come out yet.* I think that was his next step.

GOBI RAHIMI I read the *Live 2 Tell* script Pac wrote.† It was great. It had some amazing plot points, a good story arc. The characters were really well developed. I think it

Bullet (1996) and *Gridlock'd* (1997).

†An original screenplay written while Tupac was in prison about a young man who escapes a troubled upbringing by becoming a ruthless drug dealer.

was a hit. I actually, at one point after he died, had gotten an investment group to come up with $10 million to make it, but, unfortunately, the legal team that was running the estate at that point kind of put the kibosh on it.

Tupac the rapper was more of a well-refined character. As a script writer, he was able to flex all his narrative creativity in writing characters or scenarios—so sensitivity, vulnerability, all of that was very easy for him.

BECKY MOSSING I don't think there was a ceiling for him. My concern would have been that people would have pigeonholed him. Because people—his management, maybe—would have pushed him to pursue certain roles. There's such a stereotype with Black men in Hollywood of the kind of roles that they have been allowed to play. I don't know if he would have been allowed to have moved against stereotypes. If he had been given the opportunity to play a Shakespearean character, oh my god—what the world would have seen. His ability to express himself in verse was wonderful. I think that given the right role, the right director, and if a studio would have taken a chance on him, I think the world would have seen some magic. Maybe he could have reinvented himself.

RICHARD PILCHER I joked with him some years later, when he came back to visit after he started becoming very well known, that we should do a production of *Hamlet*. I'd love to direct him in *Hamlet*, and, you know, maybe we could make that happen. Blah, blah, blah. More of a joke than anything else. But the truth is, he would have made a very good Hamlet.

KARL KANI I definitely saw Pac doing more movies and becoming a mega, mega, mega star. I know he enjoyed acting. I know that many people wanted to do movies with Pac. I kind of saw Tupac getting big on the fashion scene. He was headed in that direction. He's definitely a philosopher. He was the future. He was the leader that's so missing right now. I think the whole face of hip-hop would have been different if Tupac was alive. He'd check so many rappers for not being down for the culture, not speaking up for Black women. The game would've been different. When Tupac spoke, people listened.

NAHSHON ANDERSON There were so many people that respected him and looked up to him, and loved him. And for me, I'm forty-two, and the impact that he had on my life—I'm still in the field of work that I want to be in, and to a degree, it's because of him giving me that head start. Even though he was a hard-core, you know, gangsta rapper or whatever, I would say he was just as smart as Obama. He obviously wasn't going to be the president, but he definitely would have been able to move more younger people in the right direction.

KARL KANI Tupac, he's one of the main reasons why my brand is still the number one streetwear brand in Europe right now—because they worship him like a god. Once the internet hit, and now, all these kids in Germany, Japan, can start googling and seeing what he's wearing over a period of time, that's when it really started to happen. You feel me? That's when the power of Tupac started to really, really happen—when people was able to get on the internet and do research themselves. That's when they really saw the impact that he had and what he used to wear.

BLU You can see his contribution to this life in his short twenty-five years, how big his impact on this world was. Everything that he represents, I champion, I put on a pedestal. There's no way anyone can sit in a seat and think that they can compare themselves to Tupac. I realized that there was someone out there that represents being fearless.

LEVY LEE SIMON A lot of people talked about the fact that he was already getting away from the gangsta rap kind of grind and more into politics, into more Afrocentric kinds of stuff to uplift and speak to people. At his core, he was political; he was a revolutionary. And I think that his work would have been revolutionary. Not only as a rapper, but also as an actor, as a writer, as a poet, as a public figure, as a speaker.

BLU Man, Tupac is the most passionate artist that I've ever listened to, let alone in hip-hop, which is a very, very competitive sport. It enabled him to become one of the best songwriters that we've ever heard. And it made him feel larger than life—like the biggest daredevil there ever was. You got Tupac blasting at unjust police officers. That's unheard of, to this day. You have Tupac laying down the law.

GOBI RAHIMI It's interesting, in retrospect. I would always see or hear Pac's anger toward the police and racism and all of that, and I thought I completely understood what Tupac was talking about, but only after George Floyd's murder, and all of these videos that have surfaced, did I really realize what he was talking about. He had a revolutionary rage. And as his mom once said so aptly, Pac would never bend his knee for anyone. I had an appreciation for him posthumously that I wish I had spoken up on while he was alive.

WENDY DAY I think he would have become a leader, provided somebody else didn't kill him or the government didn't kill him. History tells us that absolutely is not off the table. I think he definitely would have been some sort of a leader. I see a lot of him in Killer Mike. I see a lot of him in a lot of people that stand up to injustice. I look at people like Tekashi 6ix9ine and I wonder what Pac would have thought about him or how he would react to him, because I saw Meek Mill blast him and that was very Pac to me.* I definitely see Pac doing that, only not backing down. I can see him just crushing this kid.

ROB MARRIOTT 6ix9ine once said that the reason why he did the things he did was because he thought rap was real. He really thought the things that these rappers said, they actually did. Tupac was kind of like that. He took hip-hop very seriously and behaved that way to his detriment at the time, but, ultimately, to his immortality. That's what we love about him now and why he's persistent in the culture. He didn't use the filters that would keep him safe. He got out in front of that sight and just kept preaching what he believed. It was like a really conscious suicide in a way—a long five-year process where he committed suicide because he felt the message was more important.

*In February 2019, Brooklyn rapper Tekashi 6ix9ine pled guilty to gang activity, receiving a reduced two-year sentence for testifying against his associates. In response, Philadelphia rapper Meek Mill, then on probation for a questionable prison sentence, tweeted, "I don't represent that using influence to cause unnecessary drama and then get them locked up after he portrayed a gangbanger . . . kids will believe that and follow up and it's not cool . . . I got a say so when we talking the trenches so I'm speaking for us!"

JUSTIN TINSLEY What he was phenomenal at was taking that Black experience and composing it into art. The same way Richard Wright was as an author or James Baldwin was as an essayist—in terms of telling you about the conditions of his community. He's going to tell you in the most explicit way possible, because it makes you cringe, hearing it on a record; imagine living it in your everyday life.

BLU I think his being alive would be as big as a Dr. King or Malcolm X still being alive. There would be a lot more African American leaders standing for us. Tupac still represents Black power. He's an example of what many Black males should be—legally armed, legally making money, and standing by the culture like no other.

MARK ANTHONY NEAL There are these figures that have emerged historically over the last fifty or sixty years who were killed at a young age, who potentially could have been portals toward different kinds of possibilities for folks. For me in the 1960s, it was Fred Hampton.* We don't know who Fred Hampton would have been fully matured. Tupac is in that same tradition. We don't know who he's going to become yet.

I often think about Tupac as this figure, because he was into so many things. He was coming into maturity in terms of finding a way to be both a celebrity in Hollywood and in the music industry, but also was beginning to cultivate his political identity. He was still trying to figure out what that balance was going to be. Because he had this larger trajectory in history in the movement, I think most of us fully expected that he would develop some

*An activist who was the chairman of the Illinois Black Panther Party and the Rainbow Coalition. In December 1969, he was killed in his bed during a police raid. A jury ruled it a "justifiable homicide." However, in 1982, after thirteen years of litigation, city, county, and federal authorities reached a $1.85 million settlement with a group that included relatives of Hampton.

organizations or institutes that would allow us to reproduce more Tupacs.

I thought it was important to focus on the possibilities of a Tupac when we don't get to see that fully realized.
What a Tupac at forty years old might have been, who
would have been able to offer a kind of critical commentary and self-critical commentary on the rape charge that
he caught. I see all of that as something that was coming.
It was important to me to think about him as someone
who was potentially dangerous. To be able to reproduce
the next generation of young Black men in particular, but
also Black people in general, who were leaders, who were
activists, who were dedicated to a certain kind of Black
political tradition.

I know the folks who were long in the movement—
that is, Black Power and Black militancy movements in the
sixties and seventies—often talked about the fact that, as
he became more famous, there was a desire to protect
him. They realized that he was that bridge to another it-
eration of Black militancy.

KENDRICK WELLS I think personally he would not be
able to survive this time. We don't have leaders that can
say things—not in the Black community and not in the
world. I think Tupac would have succumbed to something
else.

MARK ANTHONY NEAL For young folk, so much of who
Tupac was, as a person, as an essence, as an artist, has
basically been lost and become this kind of flattened caricature of a moment in the mid-1990s.

Tupac was not a perfect being. He was someone

who was a person who was in process and in transition. There's nothing more human than being in process and in transition. So if young folks could connect to not who Tupac was but the process that he was going through, that would actually still bring them closer to who he is.

But then for me there's the question of the absences. In a documentary about his shooting, we find out [about] the friendship that he and Mike Tyson had. As you saw Mike Tyson's life unravel in the late 1990s and early 2000s, you start wondering what Mike Tyson's trajectory might have been if Tupac was still there. If Tupac and Biggie don't disappear, culturally, in '96 and '97, as they do, there's no cultural space for Jay-Z to take off. So it has ramifications in terms of who emerges as the public face of hip-hop.

Tupac is the hip-hop generation's messiah complex— much the way so many people tried to fill the void of King after his killing in '68. All kinds of figures have emerged who have become iconic figures. But Jesse Jackson never filled the void in that way. Louis Farrakhan never filled the void that way. Al Sharpton never filled the void in that way. And arguably Barack Obama never filled that void.

So we see these folks who gesture toward it. Just simply because of his visibility, the person that you think about is probably Jay-Z. But Jay-Z has achieved a level of wealth that, quite frankly, I think that Tupac would have never been interested in. And while Jay-Z has done things, besides behind closed doors, in terms of supporting movements, he was always someone who is so conscious of how his image and ideas are being marketed in the world. And that speaks a great deal, just in terms of the economics of hip-hop right now, where so many people are so successful financially that to be political in the ways that Tupac was political is risky. Now you put into question your sponsorships. Hell, that dude Travis Scott has a hamburger meal with McDonald's.

For Tupac, that would've been unfathomable. The political movement now has become about wealth. I don't want to dismiss that as not being important. But that's not the same kind of politics that Tupac was committed to. Tupac was committed to a politics that never left the street. Even as the idea of Tupac gets pushed up into the academy and museums and all these places of high culture, Tupac himself was always committed to the work on the ground.

VIRGIL ROBERTS I think he would have been one of those seminal figures. He was a huge pop icon. But it's so hard to say. He was in his nascent form, but he was a smart kid. He was well educated. You hear it in the lyrics he wrote and in the songs that he did. He had a worldview. But he also had a death wish. I don't know that he would have become *more*.

Sometimes when folks die young it's in part because of the way they live their lives. Maybe they can never become old. Tupac lived on the edge all of the time. That probably would've never changed. It's like trying to predict the weather. So many different factors were at play. You could say, *Okay, if we could control this, and he hadn't been shot, and this didn't happen, and this didn't happen, and this didn't happen, he would have been X.* But all those things did happen. And because they did happen, it maybe made him bigger than he otherwise would have been. When you die at your peak, you become immortalized. It's easy to say, "If this person continued on this trajectory, boy, would they have been rich and power-ful and famous and the leader of movements. Yeah." But that's forgetting all the other things that affect how we end up where we are.

ANGELA ARDIS I think he was brilliant. I think that he would have been a huge vehicle for the community, pe-riod. I think everything that's going on right now, he'd have been at the forefront of that. I think if he'd had the opportunity to transform his mindset or his condition—which, I think he was in the process of trying to do that, try-ing to figure out how to balance that out—he would have been a force to be reckoned with. He could have changed the world; the world would have been his.

PUDGEE THA PHAT BASTARD I think Pac would have changed the world. I do believe he would have changed the world. I mean, he was a revolutionary, period. I think his place in life was to illuminate things that were being glazed over. It kind of made him a martyr. To come from what he came from requires a heightened awareness for a child. I think those things kind of groomed him to become a radical member of the music business.

It sounds like me just championing him, but once you knew this person . . . he was unabashedly him. If you were a sex worker, he's a guy who's gonna be like, "Even though you were a sex worker, I love you." You probably didn't want that part told, but he's still saying you're amazing. People glorify that relationship because he became this huge celebrity, but he was still a Kennedy Fried Chicken–eatin' homeboy to me. He never told me, "Yo, call Suge and I'm gonna see if I can call you." No weird stuff ever happened. He was the same raw, convicted, truthful, giving, supportive person that I always knew.

People never really focus on the mature parts of that man. He was honest as fuck, and he was receptive to criticism around his actions. Even if he didn't change them immediately, they weren't thrown in the trash. You felt like you were talking to a receiver of the signal. Yeah, he was quick-tempered. Yeah, he was spitting in cameras. But he was a reactionary individual. It's not like it was unprompted. Coming from a troubled background, a really challenging background, you've got this person who can smile, who made social commentary. I implore you to just look at this dichotomy and look at the things that pressured him into changing.

CORMEGA Some artists are great because they've worked hard. Some artists have longevity. Some artists have appeal because of their image. Some artists have appeal because of their skill. Another thing that sells, as we know, is controversy. And then you have artists that touch people emotionally.

When I think of rappers, there is no rapper that I could think of that was more emotional than Tupac. When I think of controversial rappers, there's nobody that's more controversial than Tupac. When I think about sex appeal, I've never seen love like Tupac—he had pop stars visiting him in jail. When I think about his versatility as an artist and his work ethic . . . he's been dead for so long, but there's still unreleased music floating out there, and the same guy who made "Hit 'Em Up" made "Keep Ya Head Up." To go from "Dear Mama" to "Hail Mary" is amazing.

Speaking from an artist's perspective, there are some

rappers that are battle rappers. So if you battle them as an emcee, you will lose, but they don't know how to make good records. Some people know how to make good records, but they're not battle rappers. There are some people that know how to make good songs, but they don't know how to perform.

Pac could do it all. Even when you think of some of the best interviews in rap, you've gotta throw Pac's name in there. I could watch a Tupac interview right now for an hour and won't be bored. Me, being that I traveled all over, I'm privy to this: I'm seeing Tupac murals in Africa. I'm seeing the love that he gets when I'm in Russia, when I'm in England. No one gets as much love all over the world.

PUDGEE THA PHAT BASTARD He was the happiest, most jovial dancer in the world.

CHUCK WALKER *He is the perfect hero, because he represented different things for different people. For the indigenous people, he was a radical who took up arms and defended them. For more moderate groups, he was a rebel forced to fight and he didn't want to; he was a very religious man who said, "Don't touch the Catholic Church." He entered this form of incredible martyrdom. Just like any hero, there are lots of different interpretations.*

AUTHOR'S NOTE

THE NATURE of oral history is to probe the collective memory. In the classical sense, it is a discipline of preservation—making sure knowledge stored only in the mind isn't lost to time. Tupac Shakur is an interesting subject for such a practice. So much about his legacy has already been preserved. Yet, on some level, he remains an enigma.

In the traditional academic oral history, the primary purpose is to chronicle, for the sake of shared truth and posterity. The idea is that a number of overlapping perspectives can create a more complete picture. As an oral history, *Changes* does seek to chronicle the life of Tupac Shakur, but in no way does it seek to be a completist work. Pac is among our most well-studied figures—there is already an authoritative documentary (*Tupac: Resurrection*), a sharp critical evaluation (*Holler If You Hear Me*), an exhaustive record of his life and career (compiled by *Vibe*), and a biopic (2017's *All Eyez on Me*). There are forums, and fan sites, and podcasts. Instead, this oral history had greater interest in uncovering the man beneath the myth. It is a retrospective examination of influence. It quickly became a balancing act: Where to provide insight versus where to provide clarity? When should one person recount personal experience and when should a group rehash a public spectacle?

Many of the key participants in this story are already dead. Many who are still alive hold their memories too close to share. Some are wary of how Tupac has been portrayed in the past; others have simply said all they have to say in the twenty-five years since his death. Some are saving their stories for books they hope to someday write themselves.

My editor and I made several choices early on: that we would only include original interviews, save for the occasional explanatory footnote; that we would not exhume quotes from the dead (again, except in a few cases to provide context); and that we would let the characters themselves, their interplay and even their occasional contradictions, build out the oral history's narrative arc. Furthermore, I decided to focus particularly on those who hadn't spoken as much or could provide a rarely heard perspective. I hoped that a wide-ranging cast of characters, with differing relationships to Tupac and his work, might highlight so many aspects of his personhood that we might begin to understand him better. This is a book that yearns to provide a new frame of reference. Perhaps by seeing him through the eyes of those who knew and studied him, we might get a truer sense of who he was and how he became the paragon for so many things.

This oral history is less about all-inclusive, full-scale documentation and more about texture—about getting to the heart of what Tupac meant to people, how his life came to reflect so many different truths. I wanted to explore the many ways people saw him and how these approximations of the man came to make up a holistic depiction; how little gestures and individual stories build up over time to shape a life's arc and impact.

ACKNOWLEDGMENTS

THANK YOU, first and foremost, to everyone who participated in this project. Thank you, Sean Manning, for being there with me every step of the way and helping me see this thing through. Thank you, William LoTurco, for your support and guidance. Thank you to my mother for the endless encouragement; to my father for all the nudges back onto the path; to my aunt for the enthusiasm. Thank you to my brothers, Charles and Kristian, and my sister, Danielle; everything I do, I do with them in mind. Thanks to E, and James, and Stephen, my sounding boards. Finally, thank you to Tupac Shakur, for all that he showed us.